THE MYSTERY OF ANGKOR WAT

Amid the tangled jungle vines of Cambodia lies a splendid city of temples so wonderful that they are said to dwarf the marvels of Egypt, Greece and Rome. But behind them lies a mystery that no-one has been able to solve.

Henri Mouhot, a French naturalist, who re-discovered the temples in 1861, said they were the most important monuments that the past has left us.

1

The tough, jungle fighters of the Vietcong, who spearheaded attacks from the north in the Vietnam war a few years ago, hacked their way through the almost impenetrable forests of Cambodia, an ancient kingdom in Asia.

Their bodies shining with perspiration in the jungle heat, they wriggled almost unseen between the dense vines and thick vegetation that cloaked the Cambodian forest.

Suddenly they stopped. Before their eyes in a clearing arose an astonishing stone building, so immense that its grey battlements seemed to stretch as far as the eye could see.

Five towers pointed skywards above terraces and galleries, whose magnificence the Vietcong did not pause to admire. They had reached the temple of Angkor Wat, the most splendid building in a city of temples so wonderful that they are said to dwarf the marvels of Egypt, Greece and Rome. More than two hundred monuments in stone, their large towers covered with sculptures, stand amid jungle vines whose tentacles probe deep into the ancient stone.

But the Vietcong had not battled through the jungle to admire the creations of an earlier generation, nor to deplore the destructiveness of nature. They had arrived to use this city of temples as a base from which they could extend the territory gained in their fight against their enemies.

Amid such beautiful temples, they reasoned, they would be safe from bombing planes. They were probably right, for at the time of writing no bombs had fallen on the beautiful creations in stone. In peace, explorers may, once again, be able to visit this strange city in the jungle.

Perhaps, like Henri Mouhot, a French naturalist who re-discovered these temples in 1861, they will spend days exploring not only the temple of Angkor Wat, but also the scores of other buildings half-hidden in the jungle. Mouhot excitedly wrote that here were "perhaps the grandest, the most important and the most artistically perfect monuments the past has left to us".

Mouhot had found the vast remains of the capital of the Khmer Empire. Once this had occupied an enormous territory extending from the Gulf of Siam to the South China Sea. Within it was all of present-day Cambodia, Laos, Vietnam and part of Thailand, and it represented one of the most highly advanced civilisations South East Asia has ever known.

For six hundred years, the Khmers ruled and

Top: Indra, the god of rain on his three-headed elephant; a detail from a temple called The Citadel of the Women.
Left: framed by the roots of a banyan tree, the face of a god looks out from the gateway of the temple of Ta Som.

extended their empire until, in 1432, they suddenly disappeared. They left no records, apart from the temples in stone; and our knowledge of them comes from legends and fables.

The ruins of their cities and temples cover over forty square miles of the Cambodian forest. And the greatest of these is Angkor Wat, built by King Suryavarman II in the twelfth century as his own tomb. This stands in a walled enclosure, surrounded by a moat crossed by causeways.

It is an oblong, 796 feet long and 588 feet wide and rises 250 feet above the foundations. Five pagodas give it an air of eastern magic. In the temple are a thousand yards of sculpture on which hundreds of thousands of figures are represented with surprisingly little repetition.

Mirrored in the moat are the towers and galleries of Angkor Wat which was built in the twelfth century by King Suryavarman II as his own tomb. The temple stands in a walled enclosure and the moat is crossed by causeways.

When Edmund Candler, a travel writer, visited the temples some years ago he found that the jungle vegetation had spread to the inner courts of the temple. "One could see the roots at grips with the masonry," he wrote. "A block was overthrown here, and there a pillar wrested from its portico."

The city of which Angkor Wat is the central glory is spread over miles. "The grandeur of the shrine is repeated in fragments," wrote Candler. "Stumbling through the thick, tropical tangle, one comes upon a tower with a human face. One creeps through crumbling galleries, scrambles over fallen pillars and, in the struggle to keep one's feet, finds oneself clasping the knee of an elephant or the waist of some grotesque Hindu goddess."

In 1907, the French Government, for whom Cambodia was a protectorate, began clearing away the undergrowth from the shrines. Archaeologists continued the work after Cambodia became independent in 1955. A French scholar, Bernard Groslier, was in charge of the operation.

His plan was to dismantle the monuments and rebuild them, stone by stone, on reinforced concrete foundations saved from flooding by drainage pipes. This was necessary for the protection of the stonework from the great tropical heat and heavy rain which began to erode the stone when it was no longer guarded by the jungle vegetation.

Among the achievements of Groslier and his colleagues is the re-creation of a causeway, which is 120 feet long. Lined along it on each side are 54 giant statues, many of which were rescued from a moat into which they had fallen.

But the spread of the Vietnam war to Cambodia, and the occupation of fabulous temples by the Vietcong as a jungle sanctuary, brought this work to a halt. However, this Khmer capital was no stranger to war.

To keep their town affluent, the Khmers went to war at frequent intervals and returned with entire nations of chained slaves to hew and quarry the rock for their buildings. Two hundred thousand elephants were trained to carry the warriors and their weapons into war. Machines were made to fire arrows. Their navies rode in canoes through which arrows could not penetrate, and they had huge armies.

All this is told in the inscriptions in stone. But archaeologists have also learned that the Khmers planted widespread rice fields. Not only did they make a network of roads, but they dug dykes and canals to carry water from a natural lake to irrigate their fields.

And then suddenly, after an attack by the Siamese in 1431, the Khmers disappeared. Nobody really knows why. One theory is that a great plague wiped them out. Another belief is that their city was not capable of being defended against the Siamese, who had risen against them. Yet another possibility is that the slaves turned in revolt against their masters, massacred them and plundered the city.

The mystery lies unsolved amid the tangled jungle vines of Cambodia.

Buddhist pilgrims still visit Angkor Wat and regard it as an important centre of their religion.

4

AFLOAT OVER AFRICA

From their vantage point in the sky, Anthony Smith and his companions were able to explore Africa in a manner possible to no man before them.

Lake Manyara in Central Africa was a killer. Anthony Smith knew that as he gazed through the wicker floor of the basket, suspended from a balloon, at the lake's bouncing waves below him.

Manyara was a killer because it was a caustic lake. Inland basins like this, with no outlet into the sea, dissolve chemicals from the soil during the millions of years of their existence. Most pick up salt and become more buoyant. Lake Manyara, however, consisted of a solution of soda.

As he looked down at the lake six thousand feet below him and saw its surface streaked with soda, Smith prayed that a wind would arise to blow them clear of the thirty miles by ten miles of blistering liquid. There was very little ballast left. They could not afford to jettison any to gain increased height,

because that would be needed to control their final landing.

Whether this would be in the lake or on the far shore was up to the elements. If they landed in the lake, Smith knew what would happen. The soda would attack their eyes first, and then their skin. What would happen after that was guesswork, for nobody had swum in the lake long enough to find out.

Fortunately, after they had hovered over the lake for an hour or so, a gentle wind began to blow them clear of the lake and they made a successful descent on to dry land.

Fear is the balloonist's companion, but it was not in pursuit of danger that Smith and his two companions, Alan Root and Douglas Botting, were

floating over Africa in a balloon. They had two reasons. One was to observe and photograph the wonderful wild life that roams the plains of Central Africa. The other was to bring to life a fantasy by Jules Verne who, in "Five Weeks in a Balloon", which he wrote in 1862, sent his hero, Dr. Samuel Fergusson, on an aerial exploration of Africa.

One of their most thrilling adventures occurred when they flew over Serengeti National Park. This is a plain which spreads over nearly five thousand square miles. Centuries ago, it was levelled by the repeated flooding of Lake Victoria, which lies on its western border.

On this plain roams an enormous herd of wildebeest, which are large antelopes more familiarly known as gnus. So vast are these herds that they devour their pasture with such thoroughness that they must constantly be on the move to find fresh grass to eat. For the same reason, the Masai tribesmen also drive their cattle from one grazing ground to another. Between them, the wild animals and the cattle can tear up all the vegetation, leaving behind them an expanse of barren land.

Only from the air can one get a complete picture of the problem, of the gigantic size of the wildebeest herds and of their thoroughness in devouring every speck of growing greenery.

When Smith and his friends hovered in awe above a sea of these animals, they found that the sight was magical. "To both sides there were ten miles of animals," wrote Anthony Smith in his book *Throw Out Two Hands* (Allen and Unwin). "To the front of us and to the back, there were thousands of them. And above them all we floated with the simplicity that only a balloon can possess."

Upwards from the herd there rose a loud noise of grunting wildebeest, like the sound of a swarm of bees, but lower in note and far greater in volume.

"It was a raucous vibration coming from everywhere," wrote Smith. "It was a herd, and it was careering, walking, eating and galloping on its way. It was magnificent."

When the herd had passed, the earth on which they had marched and eaten was hard, dry and down-trodden. A few animals were standing around the muddy edge of a water-hole, which was nearly dry.

Serenely, the balloon drifted along at two hundred feet. The hot air rising in a haze from the barren patch around the water-hole was a warning that the gentleness of their flight was about to end.

As they hit the rising hot air, the balloon shot up from two hundred to 1,500 feet.

From then on, Smith and his companions had a constant tussle with the erratic air. Frequently, their balloon landed in the vast park, and they threw out several pounds of sand at a time to gain height again. Sometimes, it was necessary to adjust a valve which released hydrogen from the balloon so that they could come down to a lower altitude. Their balloon, as big as a five-storey house, had a capacity of 26,000 cubic feet, but it showed that it could behave as boisterously as a toy ballon.

Finally, after they had bounced on the ground for the twentieth time, Smith decided that is was time to land. The turbulence was doing what it liked with them. What made up his mind for him was a sudden descent from three hundred feet at the end of which they hit the ground with a painful jolt, although they

jettisoned large quantities of sand to reduce the speed of descent.

Their efforts shot them into the air again, but Smith decided to land once and for all. He turned the valve to let out a little of the hydrogen. "Hang on. I'm about to rip. Ripping now," he said. He pulled the rip lines and the hydrogen escaped to freedom.

The basket landed gently and did not even bounce. And Smith and his comrades stepped out at the end of their adventure.

Previously, they had drifted over a huge tropical forest and seen buffalo, reed-buck (antelopes) and hippos, many other kinds of animals plus a myriad of birds.

Once, over a lake in Tanzania, they saw thousands of pink flamingoes feeding or moving along the shore in long streaks. Giraffes strolled out of a wood and wandered across to the water. One walked into it and stood drinking with his legs wide apart.

Then, further on, they saw elephants and buffaloes. They were in a triangle of land reaching back from the lake and walled in by high cliffs on two sides.

None of the animals was alarmed by the balloon. Rhinos did not even raise their tails. Gazelles remained calm. Zebras cropped the grass unperturbed.

But the most exciting of all was the sight of the huge herd of wildebeest. "I had never imagined the world could be quite so full of animals," said Smith afterwards.

The sights that he saw are rarely seen from the air. Although Africa has been observed from helicopters and aeroplanes, the noise of their engines inevitably drives away the animals in fright.

But a balloon is silent. The animals had no cause to fear it, even the shadow it cast did not upset them.

This advantage gave the balloonists a wonderful vision of Africa and its wildlife which few are permitted to share.

7

FROM his vantage point high in the crow's nest of a Dutch sailing vessel, a lookout spotted a smudge of green near the horizon.

His cry of "Land ho!" sent the crew scurrying across to the starboard rail. Admiral Roggeveen looked, too. Then he excitedly consulted his charts. No land was marked at this point in the Pacific Ocean.

As the ship approached and circled the island, the Admiral noted that it was thirty to forty miles in circumference and roughly triangular, with a mountain at each corner.

Admiral Roggeveen inked on his map the triangular blob of land, and wrote beside it "Easter Island". For it was Easter Day, 1722.

Little did he know as he brought his ship to the coast that he had named the world's most mysterious island.

Roggeveen's own report sets the scene: "This island contains about six thousand souls. And all over the island stand huge idols of stone, the figure of a man with big ears and the head covered with a red crown."

One can imagine how that report intrigued other adventurers. Many made landings. They tramped the island and counted the statues. There were 230 standing all over the place. And apart from size—varying from fifteen to thirty-five feet high— the statues were all identical.

Legless, they rose from the earth at hip level. The faces were

STONE GIANTS of Easter Island

Behind the blank stares of hundreds of identical statues that watch over Easter Island lies the legend of a much loved king and a strange race of long-eared invaders.

expressionless, with receding foreheads, tight lips, prominent chins and a curious tilt at the end of the nose. But more curious still were the ears. Long and thin they hung down to the jaw. On each statue was a hat-like crown of red stone.

About a hundred of the statues stood on and around the slopes of a dead volcano. The rest adorned either side of a five-mile long avenue—the sacred road to the island's burial ground.

They had been carved in an unusual manner. Instead of first hacking out a block of stone and

All over the island stand huge statues of stone varying in height from fifteen to thirty-five feet.

then shaping it, as any of our sculptors would have done, the Easter Island sculptor had chiselled his statues into the living rock. Only when it was complete was the statue separated from the rock behind and below.

Then it was dragged to its chosen position and slipped into a hole already prepared for it. This in itself was a Herculean task, for each statue weighed between 20 and 40 tons.

Whom do they represent? Why are they there? Why are there so many? Who made them? Questions like these were expected to be answered when explorers discovered that the natives of Easter Island had 67 stone tablets covered with writing. The only trouble was that none of the natives could read them. Nor could the language experts of the civilised world.

So, for the answers to those baffling questions, scientists studied the islanders' legends, which had been handed down by word of mouth for centuries. This is how their story goes:

"Many years ago, there was a fair country called the Kingdom of Maraerenga. The king had two sons named Ko and Hoto Matua. When the old king died, Ko became king of Maraerenga and Hoto Matua was forced to flee and find a kingdom of his own.

"He set out with a fleet of canoes, carrying his wife, his followers, servants, seeds and tools. At last he came to this fertile island which he named Rapa Nui. The people prospered and multi-

plied and Hoto Matua wore the crimson crown and cloak of kingship.

"His followers, all aristocratic, long-eared people, and his servants and workers, who were short-eared like us, were happy. But when Hotu Matua died, the long-eared rulers used the people cruelly and made them slaves.

"So the people rose up and killed the long-eared ones. All of them. But they remembered Hotu Matua with love, and a sculptor named Rapu was inspired to make a statue of him. When they saw it, the people were so overjoyed that they asked for more statues of their beloved former king, to keep their island safe in case other long-eared people should take revenge."

But if this legend is true, Rapu must have lived about three hundred years. For, quite apart from the 230 standing statues, there are 157 more in the quarries in various stages of construction.

They are even bigger than the standing statues, but, of course, identical in appearance. All the 157 were worked on at the same time when, for some unknown reason, the project was so suddenly abandoned that tools were left lying all over the quarries.

No one man could have done the job. There must have been a small army of sculptors and a large army of labourers, the experts now believe.

Again, in the burial ground are the bones of many more people than the island could have supported, even allowing for the tombs having been used for many centuries.

Both these facts point to the conclusion that Easter Island must at one time have been near to a much larger island, or a series of islands. Some scientists believe that Easter Island was the holy land and cemetery for its bigger neighbour.

In 1576, a navigator named Fernandez reported the existence of a large area of land not far from where Easter Island was later discovered. A ship's captain named Davis also saw this extensive land mass a hundred years later. He did not delay his voyage to land, but named the place Davis Land.

Where is Davis Land today?

It has vanished. Some natural calamity—an undersea volcanic eruption, a tidal wave, an earthquake—probably destroyed it.

Some people believe that the Easter Islanders came originally from Peru in about the year 500 A.D., where the ruling aristocracy were called Long Ears.

The many expeditions that followed a famous Routledge Expedition in 1919 have found an increasing number of statues overthrown and mutilated by the natives.

Why they do it, they will not say. They just repeat the legend of Hotu Matua. But why, believing such a legend, do they hate the statues?

If only those 67 stone tablets could talk!

But even that would not be much use now, for the natives have hidden them all so well that years of digging has failed to uncover them.

All that scientists can work on are the copies that were made of a few of the tablets before they vanished. So far, their message has been a complete blank—as blank as the stares on the identical faces of those hundreds of Long Ears that watch over mysterious Easter Island.

Easter Island, discovered by Admiral Roggeveen on Easter Day, 1722.

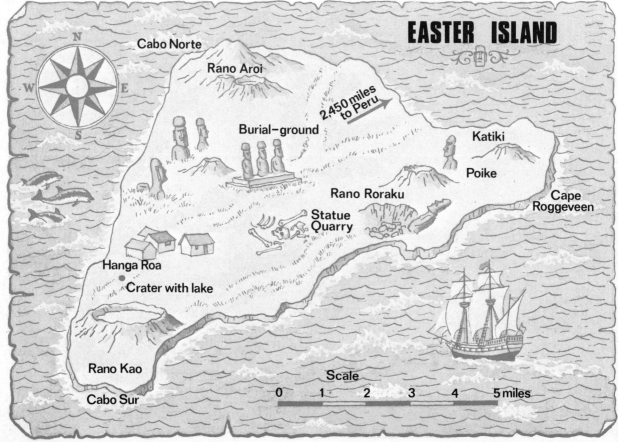

The wild and beautiful Congo held its terrors for the little people of the forest. But for a white woman and her husband—strangers in a Stone Age civilisation— the delights far outweighed the dangers.

LIFE AMONG THE PYGMIES

Mademoiselle, a basenji dog, was curled up on a raffia mat beside the bed of her mistress, Anne Putnam. In the corner of the room, a baby chimpanzee dozed in her cage.

The night was peaceful in the middle of the Ituri Forest on the banks of one of the Congo's tributaries in the heart of Africa.

Anne Putnam had fallen asleep while writing a letter. Outside, the forest was still. No sounds came from the small compound of buildings owned by Anne and her husband. Nothing stirred in the small hotel, hospital and zoo which they ran

Lent strength by her terror, Anne broke open the cage and grabbed the chimpanzee by its collar.

From her first visit to one of their villages, Anne grew to like the pygmies and became their friend. They were the smallest people in the world and their lives were still simple and primitive, although they lived less than a mile away from a great highway which crossed the continent of Africa.

close to the geographical centre of Africa.

A whimpering from the dog awoke Anne. She roused herself to hear the chimpanzee chattering in fright. Something rustled in the dried leaves of the roof of her home and scampered down the hard mud wall. It was a scorpion. Other insects began scampering away.

"What's bothering them?" thought Anne, as she swung her feet over the edge of the bed.

Her answer came from Abazinga, the animal keeper who pounded on the door of the house and shouted, "Madami, if you'd live, get out of the house."

Anne hurried into her dressing gown and slippers just as Abazinga burst into the bedroom. "Bwana sent me, Madami," said Abazinga. "The ants are here. We must go."

In a flash, Anne understood the mad scuttling of the vermin and the unrest of her two pets.

Somewhere in the forest a column of blind driver ants was relentlessly marching towards them. Their quest was for food—living food, because they are carnivorous. Other species of ants, spiders, beetles and caterpillars are their main prey. But they also eat small mammals. "Nothing gets away that cannot run or fly," one of the pygmies from a nearby camp told Anne.

So deadly are these ants, that in Central America, the Aztec Indians bound their sacrificial victims to stakes in the path of armies of these miniature killers. After the insects had passed by, nothing remained of the unfortunate victims but their skeletons.

Outside, by the light of torches and lanterns, natives were moving the animals from the stockade to safer quarters. Food was taken far from the hotel just before the ants began swarming through a fence.

A column of them, more than a foot wide, marched straight towards Anne's house. As they began swarming up its walls, Anne suddenly heard her chimpanzee chattering madly and remembered that she had left it locked in its cage in her room.

Thinking only of the helpless animal and not of herself, Anne rushed into the house and found the chimpanzee crouched in the corner of its cage, whimpering in fear.

The cage had no locks, but the African carpenter had given it latches that a monkey's fingers could not open. As she tugged at them in her terror, Anne found that they defied her fingers too. After a while, however, she managed to undo all the latches but one.

Meanwhile her husband, Pat, who had an injured leg, was limping into the house to help her. But while Anne was tearing at the last fastening, she felt a sudden pain in her leg as if she had been struck by a dart. It was an ant bite and it hurt like a wasp sting. Then came another . . . and then more.

Lent strength by her terror, Anne wrenched at the final fastening, broke it and ripped open the cage door. Grabbing the chimpanzee by the collar, she ran outside to safety, only to learn of a disaster. Someone had taken a genet out of the stockade, thinking they were moving it to safety, and tied it to a stake which proved to be in the path of the ants. "It cried like a kitten, Madami," said an African servant. "But it was too late to do anything."

When the ants had passed by, after almost two hours, the genet was a skeleton, its bones cleaned of every morsel of meat.

"Standing there in the eerie flare of the torches, I hated the Congo and its merciless ways as hard as I could hate it," said Anne afterwards. "It was a green Hell, full of latent evil, overpowering in its brutish heartlessness."

But when Anne entered her home later, she found nothing amiss, apart from two things. A cup which held palm oil had been drained dry, and the leopard skin part of a pygmy dance mask had been eaten away. Nothing else showed that her house had been raided and examined by thousands of tiny ants.

This experience is one of many exciting incidents which Anne Putnam describes in her book, "Eight Years With Congo Pigmies", published by Hutchinson & Co. Ltd., and as a paperback by Panther.

The establishment she ran with her

husband consisted of a hospital, which was operated in conjunction with the Belgian colonial government for the natives. There was a small hotel, the revenue from which helped to pay the hospital's expenses, and cottages with room for eight or nine guests, which were her responsibility. Added to this were a small house and a small zoo.

Camp Putnam was the name of this establishment, which was on a river's edge deep in the jungle and surrounded by native tribesmen.

Less than a mile away was a great highway which crossed the continent from Algiers on the Mediterranean to Cape Town. Along this road came the travellers who stayed at Camp Putnam. Some were wealthy people hunting with professional guides, some were film units on location and others were hard-up adventurers exploring the great continent.

✳ ✳ ✳ ✳

What amazed all of them was the fact that a large number of pygmies, the smallest people in the world, lived in little villages all about the camp.

From her first visit to one of their villages, Anne grew to like the pygmies and became their friend. She was enchanted by her first sight of these little people. "I saw seventeen little huts, built in a horseshoe, around a central patch of grass," she wrote. "The huts, of shiny green leaves on bent saplings, were no taller than I was and had only a single opening. In front of them were pygmies, some cooking over fires, some pounding bark cloth on smooth logs and others just lolling about at ease."

After she had made several visits, the pygmies accepted her with ease, and she was able to watch their dances and their ceremonies, one of the few white women to have this opportunity.

Once they brought her a baby, whose mother had died. Anne brought this up as her own child. Missionaries who called at Camp Putnam promised help and soon the baby had a wealth of clothes, bed

covers, nappies, feeding bottles and sterilising equipment.

Anne says that she should have felt proud and happy, but instead she felt ashamed whenever she saw a pygmy baby, knowing how little it had. So, she started giving away extra clothes to every pygmy child and every African child under six months of age. She stopped giving things away when her adopted child possessed little more than he could wear.

Pygmies, however, value things other than clothes, for they wear little more than a strip of bark cloth about their loins. Physical prowess is one of the things they admire, and it was of this that the drums beat out a message like the rumble of distant thunder one evening.

The story they told was that Faizi, a little bearded pygmy, with an old man's wrinkled face, had killed an elephant. This was a great feat of courage, something which no pygmy had done for generations.

When he returned to his village, Faizi was a great hero. While the other pygmies crowded round, Faizi told how he had walked into the forest for three days until he had found a small herd of elephants. For

For hours, Faizi stalked the elephants waiting for his chance to capture one and prove his heroism to his people.

hours, he stalked them, waiting his chance.

He crept forward, step by step, until he was right beneath one of the elephants. Then he straightened himself, thrusting his spear deep into the animal's belly.

Trumpeting with pain, the elephant lumbered off. Faizi followed it for two days until he found the elephant dead from loss of blood.

When he had finished his description of the hunt, Faizi and the band of excited pygmies set off to collect the kill. They cut the great animal into manageable portions and brought it back to their camp. That night, they had a victory dance to celebrate.

After painting their faces with a mixture of water and ashes, and sticking bunches of leaves in their loin clothes, the men danced the story of Faizi's search for the beast and the victorious killing. Then the women joined in the dance, which went on

far into the night.

Anne's husband, Pat, was given the elephant's tusks as a memento of the great feat.

They were the trophies of heroism achieved by an old man, happy in his Stone Age civilisation, unspoilt by its contact with a few white people of the twentieth century.

On the surface, things have changed in the Congo since Anne Putnam and her husband ran their establishment. It is no longer the Belgian Congo. Since 1960, it has been an independent state. This brought political problems and rebellions and general unrest.

But it is doubtful if the pygmies, in the heart of the rain forests, were concerned by the battles for power. Their battle was the eternal one for existence. Their enemies were malaria, rogue leopards, buffaloes that ran wild in the noon-day heat and wicked-minded witch doctors who caused pain to be inflicted on the innocent because they were believed to be bewitched.

But, for all this, they were a happy people, whom Anne Putnam grew to love. "I knew I did not want to go away," she says at the end of her book. "This was my home."

THE POWER OF THE TIDES

AN avalanche of water broke on the starboard bow of the cabin cruiser, "Pioneer", lifting the bows to a precarious angle and threatening to tip the vessel over backwards to her destruction.

Her skipper, Fred Robotham, seized the throttle, opened it, and put the wheel a-starboard. The engine spluttered and stopped.

It was a pitch-black night, the rain was pelting down, and the River Severn in the west of England was at its wildest. Robotham was attempting to take his cabin cruiser through the Severn bore, a mighty tidal wave which rushes inland against the flow of the river. He was not undertaking the enterprise for thrills or excitement, but because his vessel would have been smashed had he left it moored to the bank.

He had spent a tiring day undertaking a hydrographic survey for the River Catchment Board,

and he knew that a bore was expected at five past ten that night. Soon after nine, he and his small crew left their berth in darkness to take up their position in mid-river. But in the blackness of the night they mistakenly found themselves too near to one of the banks.

They were in the worst position possible to ride the bore which struck them with considerable force. However, Robotham's quick reaction in opening the throttle, although the engine quickly died, was enough to save them. The bows came down, the stern lifted and they were washed through the seething crest to smash broadside into the second wave, which rolled the boat on to its side. Robotham hung on numbly as the boat rolled waterlogged and crippled, adrift in the racing tide.

By dawn, however, Robotham had repaired the engine and all was well.

The bore is a strange natural phenomenon. It occurs when a river empties into a funnel-shaped bay. If the slopes of the river bottom are just right and the tide sufficiently high, sea water may sweep up the river as a huge wave, three or more feet high. It creates an amazing and astonishing spectacle, a flashing, sparkling, wall of water that flows inland until its force is finally spent.

There are between 250 and 260 bores on the River Severn each year—two a day on about 130 days of the year. But the Severn bore is puny compared to that which flows up the mighty River Amazon in Brazil. Called a *pororoca*, this sometimes reaches a height of twelve feet.

The mouth of the Amazon is 170 miles wide. Spread over a hundred miles is a belt of half-submerged islands and shallow sand banks, and it is here that the bore begins. A roar signals its approach, and this grows increasingly louder as it advances up the river at from ten to fifteen miles an hour in the form of a breaking wall of water from five to twelve feet high.

Bores are one of the most spec-

A violent whirlpool off the Lofoten Islands was once reputed to be so dangerous as to mean certain death to any sailors caught in its eddy.

16

Spring tides (above left) occur when the Sun and the Moon are in line and cause a strong gravitational pull to be exerted upon the Earth. When the Sun and Moon are at right angles to the Earth (above right), the tides are at their lowest and are called neap tides.

A roar signals the approach of River Amazon's bore, called a *pororoca*, which sometimes reaches a height of twelve feet as it races up the river.

tacular aspects of tidal behaviour But the tides themselves are, in a way, strange and mysterious because they are caused by unseen power from the Moon and the Sun.

This power is gravity. Both the Sun and the Moon possess it, and although the Sun is the bigger of the two and its gravity is greater, the Moon's nearness causes it to exert the major influence upon our tides.

Evidence of this is seen in the regular recurrence of high tides every 12 hours 25 minutes. These are caused by the fact that at such intervals each part of the Earth faces either towards the Moon or away from it. Parts facing the Moon receive a strong pull and those away from it experience a pushing effect.

When the Sun and Moon are in a straight line with the Earth, the gravity of both these bodies is combined. Tides then rise higher and are known as spring tides. These are the times of the new or full moon. Midway between the new and full moon, when the Sun and the Moon are at right angles to the Earth, the tides are at their lowest and are called neap tides.

Apart from the rising and falling of the sea around the coasts—and bores, which have already been described—tides have other striking effects. If the tidal current rushes through a narrow channel, we get what is called a race as at Alderney in the Channel Islands.

But if the channel is irregular,

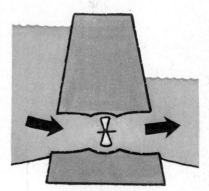
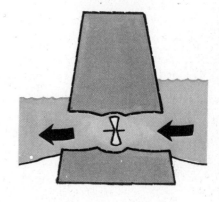

The French tidal power station across the mouth of the River Rance in Brittany generates electricity when the sea, at high tide, flows past turbines into the river. At low tide, this water is released and more electricity is generated.

the tides may cause violent whirl-pools such as the Maelstrom off the Lofoten Islands. This was once reputed to be so dangerous as to mean certain death to any sailor caught in its eddy. But, in reality, it is only so at certain states of the tide when a fierce north-west wind is blowing.

Swiftly moving tidal waters represent great power. But it is difficult to harness this for the benefit of man. An attempt to do so has been made in France where the world's first big tidal power station was built. Before this could work, a huge head of water had to be trapped behind a dam half-a-mile long, which was built across the mouth of the Rance River near St. Malo in Brittany.

Twenty-four tunnels run through the dam and mounted in each are a turbine and a dynamo. The turbines are so made that they drive the dynamos, no matter in which direction the water flows.

When the tide is rising, water rushes through the tunnels and turns the turbines. It is trapped by the dam and, when the tide goes down, the water pours out through the tunnels, again turning the turbines and generating electricity.

This current is fed into the French national grid. The object is to relieve the load on the conventional power stations during the periods of peak demand. However, the tides do not always coincide with these times. To offset this, electricity at off-peak times is fed from conventional stations to the Rance tidal station. Their power enables the Rance dynamos to operate as electric motors to drive the turbines and pump water into the basin behind the dam.

This is a way of storing electricity, for when the peak demand occurs, the water can be released from the basin through the dam's tunnels to make more power.

However, because the Rance station's operation is subject to the rise and fall of the tide, it is not as efficient as a conventional power station, because the latter is able to generate electricity continuously.

Nevertheless, if it serves to keep electric fires burning in French homes in peak periods in cold weather, it will have done its job.

An attempt to harness the tides for the generation of electricity has been made in France where this enormous tidal power station has been built across the mouth of the River Rance. Water flows through twenty-four tunnels in each of which is a turbine which drives a dynamo. In this picture, the sea is on the left and the river on the right.

Your name on the map

BY R. K. FOSTER

Personal Postmarks are found all over the world. You may be lucky enough to find yours among them

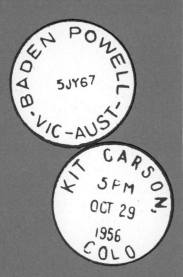

Lord Baden-Powell

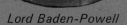

Some years ago I wrote an article about an Australian post office named Tom Price. Almost before the ink was dry a reader wrote to say, "Now there's a funny thing—*my* name is Tom Price. I never knew I was on the map!"

That experience prompted me to try another short article about a community called Norman Wells in Canada's North West Territory, and within a week or two, a letter from a flesh-and-blood Norman Wells arrived.

Personal names often pop up in geographical form, and my hobby of postmark collecting helps me to keep track of them. Mark Beech is in Kent. Edith Weston was in Rutland, when Rutland was a separate county. Mavis Enderby is in Lincolnshire and Kit Carson, named after the famous frontier scout, is in Colorado, USA.

Whenever I hear of places on the map bearing personal names I always make a point of trying to obtain their postmark. To do so is not difficult. Postmasters and correspondents around the world have been wonderfully co-operative when replying to my request —always accompanied by an International Reply Coupon—for

a clear copy of the postmark of their town.

This way I have added to my world-wide collection of 150,000 items such varied "personal postmarks" as Walter Moss, Tilly Foster, Douglas Hill, Betsy Layne, Mark Hall, Elizabeth Downs and Diana Lund.

One section of my collection consists of first-name postmarks. It includes date-stamp impressions from such places as Laura, Josephine, Sheila, Barbara, Angela, Margaret and Miranda. Represented in the boys' names section are Kenneth, Michael, Dennis, Roy, Bill, Joe, Gordon, Arnold—and hundreds more.

Another, much larger, section consists of surnames in postmark form. Here the list is endless, and I am constantly adding new ones. It ranges from the popular, surnames such as Smith, Jones Robinson and Brown to thousands of less familiar names such as Monterville, Seymour, Marriott, Modbury, Gunthorpe, Cholmondeley and Poulton.

All these, of course, are actual places on the map, and each one has its own entertaining background story.

A final group consists of postmarks from places specifically

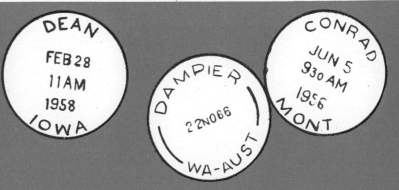

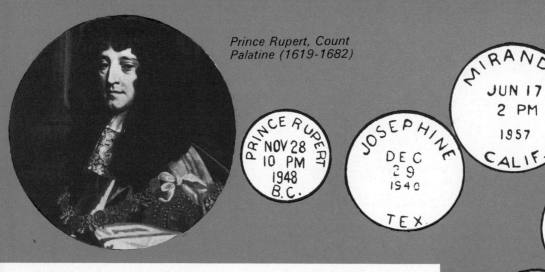

Prince Rupert, Count Palatine (1619-1682)

named for certain people. Represented here are Baden-Powell, Telford, Queen Adelaide, Prince Rupert, Churchill, Dampier and Livingstone, and many others, as well as a selection of places actually bearing both the Christian names and surnames of well-known people. In this category are Gene Autry, the cowboy film star, and William Howard Taft, a President of the United States.

The background stories to quite commonplace postmarks are almost always worth looking into.

For example, the town of Holbrook, New South Wales, Australia, was named in honour of the commander of a British submarine who was awarded the Victoria Cross for an act of gallantry during World War I. He is Commander Norman D. Holbrook, who was born in 1888 at Southsea, Hampshire.

On December 13, 1914, in command of the British submarine B.11 Commander Holbrook dived beneath five rows of enemy mines in the treacherous waters of the Dardanelles to torpedo the Turkish battleship *Messudieh*.

The force of the explosion put the submarine's compass out of action. It took nine hours of nerve-wracking underwater navigation to find a way back through the minefield to safety.

An American army officer, who died helping Kansas frontiersmen defend their homes, is remembered in the name of Culver, Kansas.

Lieutenant George W. Culver hailed from New York State and won recognition during his service with a cavalry regiment. In September 1868, trouble flared up on the Kansas frontier, and in a desperate battle at Arickaree Creek Culver was killed by redskins led by Chief Roman Nose.

Before the battle Culver had left instructions that in the event of his death his homestead claim should be given to his partner. This wish was carried out and when a town was established near the site it was given the name Culver.

Stirring stories of this kind lie behind many postal place-names. It's almost always worthwhile to inquire "How did this place get its name?" when an unusual postmark comes your way. You may even find that somewhere in the world there's a place which bears your own name—with a postmark to prove that you are really "on the map".

THE STICK THAT COMES BACK

In spite of its association with primitive peoples, the boomerang is a deadly and highly efficient weapon

IT is often assumed that the boomerang is of Australian origin. But such is not the case. Although best known as a weapon used by the Australian aborigine, the boomerang is also used by some natives of north east Africa, the tribes of southern India, and the Hopi Indians of Arizona in North America. There are also records of it being used in ancient Egypt.

The word 'boomerang' does, however, come from the aborigine language. Originally 'wo-mur-rang', the earliest printed record of its use appears in a dictionary published in 1798.

In spite of its association with primitive peoples the boomerang is a deadly, and highly efficient weapon. There are two types: the war boomerang, which is used for killing or stunning animals and, of course, one's enemies, but which does not return to the thrower, and the well-known return boomerang which, as its name suggests, does return to the thrower if it does not hit anything.

The return boomerang is sometimes used when

A boomerang that will return to the thrower, provided it does not hit anything, has been flung by this man. In his hand he holds a non-returning boomerang which is used for killing or stunning animals.

Australian aborigines, who are taught to use boomerangs almost as soon as they can walk, live in homes like this. There are also settlements of wooden huts under government supervision.

hunting birds but its main purpose is recreational. From the day he can walk an aborigine boy is taught the skills of the throwing stick. A flick of the wrist sends the boomerang spinning into the air when thrown. This spinning, the aerodynamic shape of the boomerang, and the method of throwing into the wind are the basic secrets of the art.

Formerly boomerangs were cut from a natural bend in a hard wooded tree such as acacia, but even the aborigine has succumbed to the influence of the twentieth century for most modern boomerangs are made of plastic or steel. Return boomerangs can be anything up to two feet in length, but the war boomerang was about five feet long and required the use of both hands to throw it.

Champion boomerang thrower of Australia is Bob Burwell of Slack's Creek in Queensland who has achieved a throw of ninety yards in which the flight of the boomerang was about 250 yards. For this record breaking throw he used a boomerang of vulcanised fibre made by himself and his brother Jack.

Great skill can be attained with the return boomerang. Aerobatics of staggering complexity are child's play to expert throwers such as Joe Timbery, a stocky Australian of aboriginal descent. When Joe throws a boomerang it does everything but talk.

Leaving his hand at fifty miles per hour it whips through the air, four feet from the ground, for thirty or forty yards. Suddenly, as if imbued with a will of its own, the spinning missile rises to a height of a hundred feet, describes a wide loop in the clear blue Australian sky and starts on its return journey. When it reaches Joe it hovers momentarily above his head. In a flash he jumps up and catches it—with his feet!

Other Australians, such as Professor Harvey Sutton, former principal of the School of Public Health and Tropical Medicine in Sydney, and Frank Donnellan, a Sydney printer, have done much to popularise the sport of boomerang throwing. It is now practised avidly by people in many parts of the world.

Some people have attained a mastery of the boomerang that is equal to, if not better than, the Australian aborigine. Frank Donnellan, for example, can make his boomerang describe figure of eight loops or hover like a hawk. He can even throw it, like an Australian William Tell, so that on its return flight it knocks an apple off his own head!

OUR WONDERFUL
WORLD QUIZ

Now that you have read Our Wonderful World section, see how much you can recall of the articles printed there by answering the questions below.

1. What is the name of the tidal wave which rushes inland against the flow of the River Severn?

2. Which country uses the power of the tides to run an electricity generating station?

3. What is a pororoca and where does it occur?

4. In what country are the temples of the Khmer Empire? What is the greatest of these?

5. A species of ant in Africa eats many living things when thousands of them march in deadly columns. What is their name?

6. When did the former Belgian Congo become an independent state?

7. When did the Khmers abandon their city of temples? What records did they leave of their achievements?

8. When did Admiral Roggeveen discover and name Easter Island?

9. What strange objects are found on this Island?

10. Who was the man who, according to legend, was Easter Island's most prolific sculptor?

11. In what state of America is there a place named after the frontiers scout, Kit Carson?

12. What should you include with your letter if you want an overseas postmark?

13. Who is the submarine commander who has a place in Australia named after him?

14. Culver in Kansas commemorates an American army hero. Who killed him?

15. What Australian weapon returns to your hand when it is correctly thrown?

16. This weapon is made in two types. Can you name them?

17. Apart from wood, what materials are used for these "throwing sticks"?

18. What was the name of the cabin cruiser in which Fred Robotham rode the Severn bore?

19. How wide was the column of driver ants that marched towards Anne Putnam's house in the Congo?

20. In what century did King Suryavarman II build Angkor Wat?

THE ANSWERS ARE AT THE BACK OF THE BOOK.

OUR WONDERFUL WORLD OF ART

Greta Bridge by John Sell Cotman is a fine example of the work of British watercolour artists.

Picture reproduced by courtesy of the British Museum

The Wonder of Watercolour

THE art of watercolour painting dates back thousands of years to ancient times. The artists of some of the world's earliest civilisations used this technique of painting with water, and, as far as we know, watercolour was Man's first method of applying colour to a surface.

Over the centuries, painting in watercolours has been used by so many English artists, that it has come to be looked upon as a purely English art form.

The work of all artists is greatly influenced by the surroundings in which they live. It is the climate of the country in which an artist lives, and works, that has a particularly powerful effect on his work. In England, the pearly, misty atmosphere and light which gives her landscapes such poetic charm, is perfectly suited to the art of watercolours. The pure,

If you would like to try your hand at painting in watercolours, the first thing you should do is to make several small composition sketches of your subject like these shown here. When you have chosen the best sketch you can then start to consider all the different ways in which you can approach the subject. Perhaps the foreground or the middle distance should be emphasised more, or perhaps you think that there should be fewer trees in the picture. You must never be afraid of departing from the original sketch, because you are painting a PICTURE, not recording with absolute accuracy a faithful record of your scene.

clear colours laid in the washes which can be produced by watercolours, can be the most effective way of capturing the mood and atmosphere of an English landscape. It was for this reasons that so many English artists painted in watercolours.

The founder of the English watercolour school was an artist called Paul Sandby who was born in Nottingham in 1725. His technique was to produce a drawing in Indian ink and pencil first, and then develop it in clear washes of simple colour. Sandby greatly influenced the development of watercolour art. By his example, artists like Sell Cotman, Sam Prout and Bonnington advanced watercolour techniques, and the geatest master of all, Turner, was to make watercolour painting worthy of a place alongside oil painting, tempera and fresco.

26

The artist has chosen composition A, with a few alterations. In picture 1 the design has been drawn out in pencil fixed with a charcoal fixative and when dry, rubbed down with an eraser, leaving a faint grey drawing. A flat blue wash for the sky area was then applied, leaving the cloud areas white. To give the clouds shape, shadows were added and the edges softened with a clean, damp brush while the blue of the sky was still wet. When dry, a final wash of blue was then applied, starting at the top and gradually softened off with a clean brush as before.

Next, light tones of colour were added to the castle, hill and foreground. The trees in the foreground and the shadowy side of the hill and castle were then strengthened. In picture 2 you can see that the artist has built up the shape by applying gradually heavier tones of colour, giving form to the trees—and gradually adding to the strength of the picture area as a whole.

Picture 3 shows the work completed, and you can see, if you compare it with pictures 1 and 2 that, by gradually building up his colour, the artist has given shape and form to his picture.

Joseph Mallord William Turner, considered by many to be the greatest artist England has ever produced, was born in London in 1775, the only son of a Covent Garden barber. He showed great talent for drawing from a very early age, and while still a young boy, sold his drawings to his father's customers.

Before he was twenty years old, Turner had travelled throughout England and Wales on sketching trips.

He had a phenomenal memory and was able to paint a scene months after he had observed it, using only a rough sketch as a guide. All his wonderful paintings of seascapes were created by his direct observation of waves. For his picture of a snow storm he put to sea in a gale and made the sailors lash him to the mast for four hours, so that he could experience the storm and later paint it. His critics described the picture as

Here is an example of a water colour drawing which has been painted on a tinted paper. A pencil sketch was first made and colour applied using pure water colours and water colour mixed with white. The highlights were put in using white only and the darker areas filled in with strong pure water colour. The tinted paper makes the transparent colour darker.

"soapsuds and whitewash". They could not understand that what Turner had painted was what he had actually seen with his own eyes—an artist's vision of poetic imagination and reality.

In his later years, Turner became obsessed with a fascination for light and in particular, its effect on water in all its many moods. All his life he tried to produce the effect of light and colour and, although many people at the time did not realise it, that is exactly what Turner succeeded in doing. His mastery of watercolour has remained unsurpassed.

Turner's work exerted a powerful influence over the European artists who began to see the possibilities of using watercolour as a substitute for tempera, a very expensive, slow method of painting in which paints had to be mixed with raw egg. Continental artists began to introduce white into the watercolour and found that they could obtain an effect very similar to tempera.

For pure watercolour work, the paper used is of great importance. Since all the colours are transparent, they depend on the paper for their 'body' and it is the light reflected through the colour which gives it the 'life' which opaque colours seem to lack. Black is not used except in thin washes, when it produces cool greys. Paper with all kinds of surfaces are used, and make a very great difference to the result. Rough, knobbly surfaces give a sparkling brilliancy and freshness, while smooth ones are best for fine detailed work.

Watercolour mixed with white is called Gouache, and this can give very interesting results. European artists discovered that Gouache is in many ways similar to tempera. It has one main limitation, colours cannot be laid on top of one another, since the action of the brush disturbs the under-painting.

THE STORM THAT INSPIRED AN OPERA

Wagner's opera 'The Flying Dutchman' was based on the legend of a phantom ship doomed to sail the seas for ever.

Richard Wagner . . . he never forgot his stormy voyage.

Richard Wagner was on the run. The young composer's debts had spiralled so fast, and his creditors were pressing him so hard, that flight seemed the only answer. So he left his post as Director of the Riga Opera House and, with his wife Minna, and their huge Newfoundland dog, Robber, took to his heels and headed for the Russian-German border.

Expecting Cossacks to catch them at any moment, they managed to slip into Germany and board a small boat, the 'Thetis', bound for London. It was August 1839.

It was a terrifying voyage. Storms battered the 106 ton vessel, gigantic waves threatened to sink it. Many of the crew regarded the fugutive as a Jonah who had brought a curse on their ship, but it finally came safely to London.

Wagner never forgot that voyage. Only a few years later it sounded in the music of his first great opera, *The Flying Dutchman*, based on the grim legend of the sea captain forced to sail the stormy seas for ever in a phantom vessel. The story had been much on his mind during the nightmare voyage.

The opera was first staged at Dresden in 1842. What a thrilling moment it must have been when the overture, whose first bars are like a raging sea, rang out in the theatre. Wagner was to write greater operas, but none more simple and direct and thrilling to audiences who did not and do not know his style. This is a short account of what happens in his version of the legend, based on an account of it he had read in a book by the poet Heine:—

★ ★ ★ ★

To escape from a storm, a Norwegian ship has anchored in a cove. Her captain, Darland, realises he

29

is still some seven miles from home and his daughter, Senta, so goes below for a rest.

Suddenly a ghost ship with blood red sails appears and anchors beside Darland's ship. Her captain is the Flying Dutchman and he sings of the curse on him. Once, in a great storm he had sworn he would round the Cape of Good Hope though Hell bar his way. The Devil heard him and condemned him to sail the seas for ever unless he is redeemed by the love of a faithful woman. Only once every seven years can he go ashore and search for one. The seven year moment has come round once again.

Darland appears and talks to the stranger, who learns he has a daughter and wastes no time in asking to marry her. Darland, seeing the treasure aboard the phantom ship, hastily agrees!

The next scene is in Darland's house, where Senta is staring at a portrait of the Dutchman, she sings of him to her friends, who are spinning. She is obsessed by the man she has never met and claims she will be the one to redeem him. Her lover Erik, who comes in with news that her father is near, gets a poor welcome.

Darland and the Dutchman appear and there is an electrifying scene when Senta and the stranger are left alone. It ends with them swearing to be faithful to each other till they die.

Disaster occurs in the final scene outside Darland's house and beside the bay where the two ships now lie at anchor. First of all the villagers, who had been having a marvellous party, are terrified out of their wits by the phantom ship and its devilish crew, then Senta appears, with Erik behind her, pleading for her love.

The Dutchman overhears them and thinks he has been betrayed. In despair, he tells Senta who he is, but she replies that she already knows and will save him. It is too late. He puts to sea. Senta runs to the top of a cliff, calls to him, then hurls herself off. The phantom ship is sucked down in a whirlpool and as the opera ends we see Senta and the Dutchman rising up to heaven. The curse has ended.

Wagner's great opera 'The Flying Dutchman' has been performed all over the world, thrilling audiences with its music and drama.

An example of 16th century stained glass work at a church in Holland.

STORIES TOLD IN GLASS

Churches and cathedrals all over the world contain some of the finest works of art man has ever produced. For centuries, artists and craftsmen have created paintings and sculptures "to the greater glory of God", and to express in visual form the beliefs and teachings of a religion.

One religious art form of Christianity which has been sadly ignored by many people over the years is stained glass windows. This is a pity because these beautiful works of art can be found in many small village churches as well as in the larger, more famous cathedrals.

Stained glass work in Europe began in 1066 during the time of the Norman Conquest of Britain, and developed rapidly throughout the following century. No one knows for sure when coloured glass was first used for windows, but the oldest examples are at Augsburg in Germany which date from about the year A.D. 1,000.

Churches during the Middle Ages were not the sombre, solemn grey stone buildings they became in later years. Arches and pillars were painted, walls were covered with murals, the woodwork throughout was carved and gilded, and everywhere was colour. Through it all shone the dramatic, mystical light of the stained glass windows with their brilliant, vital colours.

Stained glass windows at that time were not created merely for decoration in churches, although it is true they have always enhanced the beauty of church interiors. There were two reasons for their production. They taught the basic lessons of Christianity to church-goers, and they helped to instil in them a sense of spiritual devotion.

It is probably difficult to imagine what churchgoing was like to most men and women in those days when it was a very strange and bewildering affair to attend services. For one thing, all the services were in Latin or French; languages which most people could not understand. There were no books to read, and anyway only very, very few could read at that time. So there were only two ways in which churchgoers could be helped to understand the teachings of Christianity: the sermon, expressed in everyday, simple language, and the stained glass windows with their pictures depicting the life of Christ and its meaning, and stories from the Bible. This is why stained glass has always been called the 'Bible of the poor'.

As the strange, mysterious words and intonations of the priest echoed round their ears, the worshippers would sit gazing at the brilliant coloured light that shone down on them and at the pictures whose meaning they could understand. There would be pictures of saints and stories of their lives, of Apostles, and of Angels. In picture windows there would be stories from the Old and New Testaments, pictures of the Seven Works of Mercy and the Seven Deadly Sins, and in the most important position of the church, the Last Judgement or Doom Window.

The Doom windows were perhaps the most graphic and vivid of all the subjects used in stained glass work. They always followed the same general form. At the lower part of the window the souls are being judged by St. Michael. Most of them are then plunged into the torments of hell and only a few pass St. Peter and enter Heaven. It is interesting to note that many of the damned were often depicted as kings,

Stained-glass windows are a specialized production. When a design has been approved, a full-size drawing in black and white, called a 'cartoon', has to be prepared. Over this tracing linen is placed, on which each piece of glass is outlined to form a jigsaw of colour.

A

B

Cutting out the required pieces of glass (A) is the least of the glass-cutter's skills. Faced with the original colour scheme, he has to assess which of the shades at his disposal will harmonize best when the window is finally assembled.

A glass-painter (B) places pieces of glass that need detailed drawing on the cartoon and traces in the lines. The glass is temporarily fixed upright so that tones can be painted in, before final firing fuses the paint into the top surface of the glass.

In the glazing room (C) the pieces of glass are assembled together and slotted into strips of lead. A lead strip is placed between the glass sections and soldered until the entire window is formed.

popes, and bishops; showing that only the virtuous, whatever their station in life, were saved from doom.

Unlike religious paintings and sculptures produced in later years, Medieval art forms rarely have a name to them; their creators remain anonymous. Many people have always believed that it was the monks who produced medieval stained glass windows, but this was not the case. They were supplied and fitted by lay craftsmen. These men would start as apprentices in a workshop under a 'master glazer' who was a very highly-respected and brilliant craftsman. In Britain the main stained glass manufacturing centres were at London, York, Canterbury, Oxford, and other cities.

* * * *

From the 12th to the 14th century the stained glass artists worked in a simple style and, though they regarded their work as a trade for which they earned money, their first interest was to present stories of the Christian faith in the most effective and simplest way. This is why early stained glass is so beautiful and moving. Craftsmen of later years began to take much more interest in the elaboration of detail in their work. In this way, much of the meaning of stained glass was lost.

When enamel paint became popular in the 17th century artists began to imitate the effect of oil painting and this too, took away much of the charm in stained glass. Then in 19th century work we find elaborate, detailed windows, with little life or beauty in them. Large firms at this time reduced the art of the stained glass window to a mechanical, factory-type, production and in almost every window of this century this is sadly apparent.

Examples of the fine work of medieval stained glass artists have, over the years, been allowed to fall into decay. In many churches they have been replaced by poor Victorian imitations, or have been badly restored. Fortunately, this is not always the case. Some of the finest windows have been restored beautifully by patient artists who spend many years on the smallest pieces of glass to restore them to their former grace and beauty.

There are far too many examples of stained glass windows to mention all of them in this book, but some are included in the following list. These are among the most famous, but remember much of the most beautiful medieval stained glass can be found in the smallest village church.

Canterbury Cathedral, York Minster, Durham Cathedral, Gloucester Cathedral, Lincoln Cathedral, Norwich Cathedral, Worcester Cathedral, Salisbury Cathedral, Chichester Cathedral, Wells Cathedral, Winchester Cathedral, and many of the colleges at Oxford and Cambridge Universities.

C

HOW STAINED GLASS WINDOWS WERE MADE

Glass, as you may already know, is made by heating a mixture of sand, soda or lime, and potash to an extremely high temperature until they melt and mix together to become a clear, transparent material which

Liquid cement is rubbed into the cracks between the glass and lead on both sides. Then all the superfluous cement is removed and the panels left for two weeks to harden before the window is finally ready to be set up in position (right), and add to the joy of the beholder.

hardens as it cools.

To make the glass coloured, other special ingredients are added before the glass mixture melts. These are mainly metal oxides : copper oxide produces red or ruby glass, cobalt is used for blue, manganese for purple, and iron for green or bright yellow.

The way in which stained glass windows are made has not changed very much over the centuries. Today, methods are more sophisticated, but are much the same as those used by the early stained glass window makers.

The first thing which the stained glass window maker had to do was to measure the window spaces to be filled and to take templates or copies of their shape. Then the pictures were drawn on a whitewashed trestle table. Charcoal was used for outlines, red paint for flesh areas, and dark paint brush strokes were used to represent the strips of lead.

The cartoon, which is the name for this drawn design, was copied on to parchment so that it could be traced. The drawing itself was done by the master glazier. When the cartoon was finished, pieces of different coloured glass were placed over it, and roughly split into different shapes to match the drawing. The glass was then finally trimmed with an iron tool called a grozing-iron (rather like a modern wheel glass-cutter). The details were then painted in and the glass was fired in a kiln and afterwards left to cool.

After the cooling process the pieces were again laid out on the trestle table, and then fastened together with leads. When all the pieces had been joined to make a panel, a thick strip of lead was placed all round it.

In the 12th and 13th centuries windows were sometimes held in place by iron armatures, the same shape as the panels. These panels were then joined to the armatures with eyelets and wedges, and the armatures were held securely in an oak frame which ran right round the opening of the window.

In later years, supports for the panels were fixed on the inside of the glass window to prevent the wind from blowing the glass in. Vertical iron bars called 'stanchions' or 'standards' were fixed to the panel and crossed by vertical 'saddle bars'.

The Birth Of a Monster

When Mary Shelley and her friends began to make up ghost stories to pass the time during their holiday in Switzerland, none of them could have known that Mary's supernatural monster was to exercise such a fascination over people's imaginations

L ightning bathed the turrets of the grim, grey castle with an eerie light. Professor Frankenstein listened to the crackling thunder and the rain lashing the windows. At last, he felt, the conditions were right for his great experiment—the creation of life.

As Professer Frankenstein thrust open the casement window, a bolt of lightning filled the room with its brilliance, illuminating the face of a body lying upon a table.

But it was no ordinary corpse, for Frankenstein had constructed it of portions of dead bodies obtained from mortuaries. Each section had been carefully chosen so that the composite human would be superior in every way to ordinary mortals.

Beneath each ear was an electrode connected to a lightning conductor on the castle's roof. With each flash of lightning, a pulse of high power surged into the body.

Anxiously, Frankenstein watched his creation. Its face twitched. The eyes flickered open . . . it was alive ! His macabre experiment had succeeded.

Film audiences in the 'thirties watched such a scene as this with tingling spines, for the story of Frankenstein and his monster was the subject of a succession of horror films, some of which have since been shown on television.

Few probably knew that the monster was the brain-child of a woman, Mary Wollstonecraft Shelley, the wife of Percy Bysshe Shelley, the poet. One summer, early in the 19th century, she and her husband were on holiday with a group of literary friends in Switzerland. To pass the time during the long rainy days, they made up ghost stories.

Lord Byron, the poet, created a horrific tale about a vampire. Percy Shelley related spine-tingling ghost stories. A young Italian doctor frightened them all with his account of a lady with a skull for a head.

As their imaginations ran dry, the men turned to Mary for a story.

"Come," said Byron. "You have been sitting here quietly all these weeks listening to our weird imaginings. Surely you can invent your own supernatural adventure. Something that will outdo all of us."

Before going to bed that evening, Byron

The monster (left) was the brain-child of Mary Wollstonecraft Shelley (top left). The first sound version film of Frankenstein was made in 1931 with Boris Karloff (top right) realistically made up as the monster created by Professer Frankenstein (right).

and Shelley argued about the possibility of creating a human being. They felt that life could be restored to a corpse by electricity ; that a creature could be assembled and imbued with human vitality. As Mary sat listening, she realised that this was the story she would contribute to their collection of the macabre.

In her diary she wrote : "Night waned upon this talk, and even the witching hour had gone by before we retired to rest. When I placed my head upon my pillow, I did not sleep, nor could I be said to think. My imagination, unbidden, possessed and guided me . . . with a vividness far beyond the usual bounds of reverie.

"I saw the hideous phantasm of a man stretched out, and then, on the workings of some powerful engine, show signs of life and stir with an uneasy, half vital motion.

"Frightful must it be ; for supremely frightful would be the effect of any human endeavour to mock the stupendous mechanism of the Creator of the world.

"The idea so possessed my mind that a thrill of fear ran through me . . . On the morrow, I announced that I had thought of a story."

The story she then outlined to the two enthusiastic poets was the beginning of "Frankenstein" ; the novel about a man-made man that was to ensure immortality for the nineteen-year-old bride, who had previously been so overwhelmed by her husband's genius.

At first, Mary thought of Frankenstein only as a short story. But Percy Bysshe Shelley, suddenly showing more interest in her work than his own, insisted that she build a full-length book round the theme. He told her it was significant on two levels : "as a pure horror story, and as a moral tract pointing that man must never interfere with the workings of his Maker."

As soon as Mary completed the manuscript of Frankenstein, Shelley took it to a London publisher and persuaded him to publish it. Impressed by the literary merit of the work alone, the publisher promptly accepted it, and paid the then magnificent advance of £400.

If that sum of money was a fortune to the hard-up Shelleys, even greater fortunes were to be made when the Frankenstein monster made its appearance in films.

Its debut occurred in a one-reel silent film made in 1910. But it was not until the arrival of sound that the monster appeared in all its guttural, grunting horror. The title of this film was simply "Frankenstein", and it was followed by a succession of similar films, variously entitled : "The Bride of Franken-stein","The Son of Frankenstein", "The Ghost of Frankenstein", "Frankenstein Meets the Wolf Man", "The House of Frankenstein", "The Curse of Frankenstein", "The Revenge of Frankenstein", "Frankenstein's Daughter", "The Evil of Frankenstein", "Frankenstein Created Woman" and, as what seems to be a suitable epitaph, "Frankenstein Must be Destroyed".

Little could Mary Shelley and her friends making up ghost stories in their villa in Switzerland have dreamed that her super-natural monster was to exercise such a fascination over people's imaginations.

The first sound version of Frankenstein was made in 1931 with Boris Karloff realistically made up as the monster. With a padded body, an artificial skull built upon his own, and a great deal of putty applied to his features, and shoes that weighed eighteen pounds each,

Karloff lurched along the floors of the film castle with horrifying realism.

It became the most famous horror film of all time, and even inspired, many years later, a creepy cartoon series called the "The Addams Family". in which the monster appeared. Later, there came a comedy film series on TV called "The Munsters" which featured a family of weirdies, with the hero in Franken-stein monster make-up. This first appeared on BBC television in 1965.

In Mary Shelley's story, the monster escapes. Frankenstein follows it to the Arctic regions to destroy it, but is himself murdered by the monster. The monster then disappears.

That was the end of the story as far as Mary Shelley was concerned. But the creature's undecided fate left the film makers with the opportunity to resuscitate it for further adventures of horror—and this they have done with spine-chilling frequency.

One of the spine-chilling episodes from Mary Shelley's book

Put on a play

Acting can be great fun when it is done with other people, especially if you decide to put on a play of your own. It will certainly involve a lot of hard work, but you will be richly rewarded with an exciting, enjoyable experience that you will probably never forget

THE next time you sit at home feeling bored, wondering what to do, why not think about putting on a play?

Most of us love to act, and drama is such fun when it is done with other people. Acting can teach us a great deal about the world about us, the people who live in it, and how and why they behave as they do, because an actor has to observe everything that is going on about him. But above all, acting can be exciting and enjoyable, especially if

you decide to put on a play of your own.

The first thing you have to decide is the material you want to use for the play. There are so many ways of choosing a subject that you may find it difficult to make a selection. You may want to take a play by a well-known author that you already know and like. If you want to put on a classical play you could choose one by Shakespeare: *Julius Caesar, A Midsummer Night's Dream, The Tempest,* or *Henry V* would be a

good choice.

Many of the novels by Charles Dickens have been dramatised by Guy Pertwee, so you could produce one of these plays adapted from the novel. Or you may want to select some scenes from one of your favourite books and make up the script yourselves. *Robinson Crusoe, King Solomon's Mines, Huckleberry Finn, Wuthering Heights* and *Coral Island* are full of exciting scenes which you can dramatise. This method will entail much more work than simply selecting a play which has already been written, but it can be very rewarding.

Incidents in the life stories of famous people in history make very good plots for play writing. The story of Napoleon's march on Moscow, finding it in flames, and having to make the long march home in the depths of winter, is one example. Others include: Captain Cook arriving in Australia; Captain Scott's expedition to the South Pole; the final battle of the English Civil War at Preston between Cromwell's forces and the King's men.

Current affairs can provide good plots for plays too. Industrial disputes, government struggles over new laws, new discoveries and developments in transport; all these can be used as themes and written up as plays.

Once you have decided on the play, story-line or plot and, if necessary, written the script, everyone involved in putting on the play

Everyone involved in putting on a play should take part in discussions about the script, the characters, the costume and the settings. Here, a young producer of a youth theatre production goes over the script with two of the actors

should study more about its subject matter. If it is historical you will have to read books about the particular period in which the story is set; what sort of clothes people wore, and what events were happening at the time.

If the play is about a particular person or incident in history, you should try to find a book about the subject and read that too. Your public library can be a great help here, because if the play is to be successful you must always try to recreate the atmosphere and mood of the play, to make it accurate, and to achieve this, you must have some knowledge of the type of props and costumes you will need.

Once this has been done, you can then decide on who is to do what. Everyone should be able to take part both in the acting and in the technical aspects of play production.

Perhaps some of your friends are good at sewing and would be willing to make costumes for the play. Others may be skilled at woodwork and handicrafts, and they can be in charge of making the 'props'. Everyone should make use of the particular skills they have, and since play production is based on team work, every member of the group should be willing to lend a hand where it is needed.

If there are some very shy people among your friends, don't push them into the background. Encourage them to take part in everything to do with the play, including the acting. On the other hand, if there is a particularly dominating person in the group, you must not let him take over the whole show. *Every* person involved matters, whatever part he or she takes.

Once the casting has been arranged, the lines of the play must be learnt off by heart. Then the rehearsals begin. This is a very important part of play production, because it is at rehearsal time that the play really begins to develop.

The great danger in rehearsals is that they can become very boring. Don't make heavy weather of it by over-rehearsing. There may come a time, when you are all tired. Some of the actors may start to forget their lines, and it is at this point that you should take a break, and go back refreshed and ready to start again.

Every actor must learn to understand the actions, feelings and emotions of the character he is playing so that he can give a *convincing* performance. If you are playing the character of an old man, for for example, you must walk, talk, behave and feel like an old man.

Next time you see an old man—in the street or in the bus—make a careful observation of his actions. How does he speak? How does he walk? How does he sit down? Certainly not as you would. Once you begin to look around you and relate what you see with your acting, you will become much more skilled as an actor. Because as an actor you are expressing the feelings of a person, and if that character is to be convincing to an audience you must be able to portray him physically, mentally and emotionally.

After all, it is your future audience that is to watch your play, and if

your play is to be a success, your audience must be able to enjoy seeing it! This is why positioning on stage is so important. The audience *must* be able to see and hear the actors.

Costumes, settings and props are very important in recreating the whole mood and atmosphere of a play. All of them must be in keeping with the style and period of the story, but they do not have to be elaborate affairs. A few bits of furniture, well-chosen, can be just as effective as a huge, complicated set, just as a simple costume can be.

Some kinds of plays may benefit from the use of sound effects and music, and if you want to be really ambitious you could record your own sound effects for the play. Here are some excellent ways of creating sound effects:

A CROWD SCENE. The general effect of this should be a murmer or a roar. But a crowd is not well imitated by people off stage uttering vague phrases and 'hoo-ray-ray' cheering noises. If possible, each person should have some set words to say or shout and there should be a 'conductor' giving signs for the crowd to start, get louder, then softer, and finally fade away.

MARCHING MEN. This will be most effective if you choose a play with a military theme. Construct a shallow tray about six feet long and 18 inches wide from strong plywood Fill it with gravel or small pebbles. Three people marching on the gravel will sound—not like three men marching—but a PLATOON marching. To fade the footsteps, the marching men have only to tread more softly.

FOOTSTEPS. If these are meant to be on a path, a gravel tray described above can be used. If it is meant to be on a road or footpath, they can be imitated by banging the soles of a pair of heavy boots together. (Real footsteps must NOT be heard.)

HORSES. For the sound of hooves on a hard surface such as a road or cobblestones, knock two halves of a coconut shell together (plastic bowls make good substitutes). For the sound of galloping over turf, strike a hard cushion with the fist.

RAIN. Roll dried peas or lead shot in a hatbox, on top of a drum, or in a sieve.

THUNDER. For this you will need to construct a 'thunder sheet'. Use a sheet of tin about four feet by two feet, and suspend it by cords from a crossbar. The sheet can then be shaken by a wooden handle nailed on the bottom. Use a beat on a bass drum for the initial clap of thunder, then use the metal sheet for the peels of thunder.

WIND. It would be advisable to buy a recording of wind if you do not have time to make a wind machine. For this, you need a slatted wooden drum mounted on a stand so that it can be revolved. A piece of canvas is stretched over the drum and fixed to the frame on one end, and held down on the other by a weight or spring. The drum then has

WHIP

OR NOT TO BE

to be revolved by means of a wooden handle and the wind noise is produced by the scraping of the slats over the canvas.

AVALANCHES and **CRASHES.** For small falls of debris fill a large tin bucket or coal scuttle with pieces of stone and brick, and then empty it out on to a hard surface. For a sudden clatter-crash, string four or five boards together by passing a rope through a hole in the end of each and knotting them to keep them separate (like a venetian blind). When the rope is released a crash sound will be produced.

CRACKLING NOISES. For the sound of a whip or a piece of wood being broken, screw two thin strips of wood two feet long and two inches wide, either side of a flat wooden handle. Smack this against a firm object.

BREAKING GLASS. For a large amount of glass breaking, pour some broken glass from a box into a tin bucket. For smaller quantities, drop several pieces of sheet steel, six inches square, on to a hard surface.

It is always wise to have one or two rehearsals for these sound effects because they must, of course, be produced at exactly the right time during the performance. Obviously the people chosen to produce them will be those actors who are not required 'on stage' at the particular time when they are needed.

When you think that the play has been rehearsed enough, you are then ready for your 'dress rehearsal'. For this, all the sets, props and costumes must be used and everything must be set as though there is an audience in front of you. Now you no longer have to imagine that you are wearing a Roman toga, an elaborate Elizabethan costume, or a few rags, because you will actually have them on.

It is at this stage that you really understand why a knowledge of the costumes needed for the play is necessary. The tight-fitting bodice and high neck-ruff of an Elizabethan dress, for example, are a great restriction on movement. You will begin to realise why ladies in those times moved so elegantly and gracefully. With the kind of clothes they wore, they *had* to sit upright, rise from their seats slowly, and walk carefully.

When the great day for the performance of your play comes, everyone will probably suffer from nerves. 'Butterflies' in the stomach are felt by most professional actors before they go on stage. You must not worry about forgetting your lines, making a wrong movement, or making an exit before you should. If your rehearsals have gone well, a major catastrophe is unlikely to occur. But you should try to find someone who can act as a 'prompt' just in case someone does forget his lines. A prompt is someone who sits

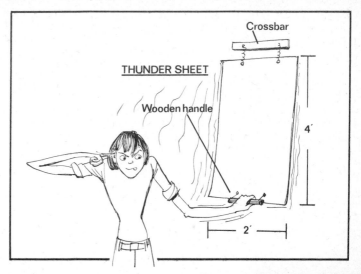

THUNDER SHEET
Crossbar
Wooden handle
4'
2'

in the 'wings' offstage, with a copy of the script before him. If anyone on stage does forget their lines, the prompt whispers his lines to him, and the play goes on. If anything does go wrong during the performance, all should carry on as though nothing is wrong. Giggling, or looking silly, looks ridiculous to an audience, so try to be as professional as you can and get on with the play.

Once the performance is over, and you have stood on stage receiving the applause of a well-satisfied audience, you will know that all the hard work and effort you have all put into the play will have been worthwhile. It is at this stage, that you can begin thinking about the subject for your next play.

You must never throw away all those props and costumes you have made. Store them away in your theatrical box—they are bound to come in useful for any future plays you put on. For when you have experienced the fun and enjoyment of putting on a play of your own, you will very likely want to do it again. And the experience you have gained from your first effort will make your next play even better.

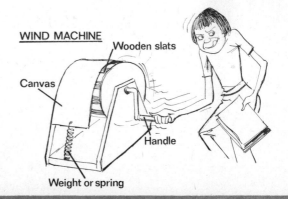

WIND MACHINE
Wooden slats
Canvas
Handle
Weight or spring

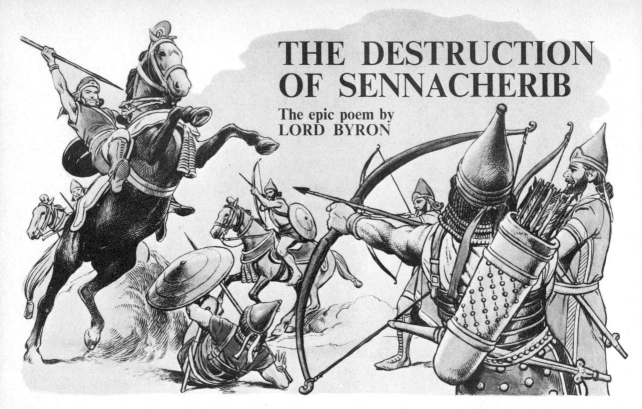

THE DESTRUCTION OF SENNACHERIB

The epic poem by LORD BYRON

The Assyrian came down like a wolf on the fold,
And his cohorts were gleaming in purple and gold;
And the sheen of their spears was like stars on the sea,
When the blue wave rolls nightly on deep Galilee.

Like the leaves of the forest when Summer is green,
That host with their banners at sunset were seen;
Like the leaves of the forest when Autumn hath blown,
That host on the morrow lay withered and strown.

For the Angel of Death spread his wings on the blast,
And breathed in the face of the foe as he pass'd;
And the eyes of the sleepers wax'd deadly and chill,
And their hearts but once heaved, and for ever grew still!

And there lay the steed with his nostril all wide;
But through it there roll'd not the breath of pride:
And the foam of his gasping lay white on the turf,
And cold as the spray of the rock-beating surf.

And there lay the rider, distorted and pale,
With the dew on his brow and the rust on his mail;
And the tents were all silent, the banners alone,
The lances uplifted, the trumpet unblown.

And the widows of Ashur are loud in their wail;
And the idols are broke in the temple of Baal;
And the might of the Gentile, unsmote by the sword,
Hath melted like snow in the glance of the Lord!

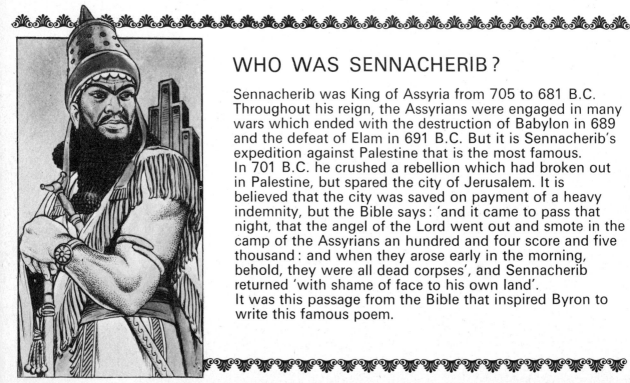

WHO WAS SENNACHERIB?

Sennacherib was King of Assyria from 705 to 681 B.C. Throughout his reign, the Assyrians were engaged in many wars which ended with the destruction of Babylon in 689 and the defeat of Elam in 691 B.C. But it is Sennacherib's expedition against Palestine that is the most famous.
In 701 B.C. he crushed a rebellion which had broken out in Palestine, but spared the city of Jerusalem. It is believed that the city was saved on payment of a heavy indemnity, but the Bible says: 'and it came to pass that night, that the angel of the Lord went out and smote in the camp of the Assyrians an hundred and four score and five thousand: and when they arose early in the morning, behold, they were all dead corpses', and Sennacherib returned 'with shame of face to his own land'.
It was this passage from the Bible that inspired Byron to write this famous poem.

THE WORLD OF MARK TWAIN

Wit, wisdom and wonderful humour bounce off the pages of Mark Twain's books. Like the life of their author, they are packed with adventure and excitement, and have delighted readers, both young and old, all over the world

It was the magical hour of midnight when Sam reached the lonely spot on the river bank where he had decided to take a swim. All that summer, a hot, stifling, sultry air had hovered among the towns of Missouri at the heart of America. Now, it clung to the young boy's clothes and untidy red hair as he sat, deep in thought, among the undergrowth.

Before him lay the mighty Mississippi, seemingly motionless now under the calm, starlit sky. Downstream stood an idle steamboat,

its huge stern paddle wheel gleaming in the moon's midnight glow. To the west lay the town of Hannibal, where young Sam lived.

The town and its people, the river and its steamboat traffic, and the fields, farms and woods that surrounded them, made up the boyhood world of Samuel Langhorne Clemens, who grew up to become Mark Twain, the writer and humourist who gave to the world the delight and wonder of the stories that flowed from his pen.

He was born in the village of Florida, Missouri in November, 1835. His father was a storekeeper and at times a lawyer, and although he had little talent for making money, Sam and his brothers and sisters did not go hungry.

Four years after Sam was born, the family moved to Hannibal, the town destined for fame because it played such an important part in Mark Twain's finest books.

Hannibal lay on the banks of the Mississippi, one of the great trade

After eighteen months learning the strange mysteries of navigating the channels of the Mississippi, Clemens obtained his pilot's licence—a dream he had cherished since childhood had come true.

routes across America. It was the Mississippi that brought to the town all kinds of colourful and exciting characters — river pilots, circus troops, minstrel show companies— all of them carefully observed by young Sam, and many of them are portrayed with wit and wisdom in the books he wrote in later years.

Sam's life as a young boy in Hannibal was a series of irresponsible, mischievous escapades. His fondness for swimming, several times led him into dangerous waters in which he nearly drowned, and it was his fascination for the river and its steamboats that led to his most outrageous act. As soon as he left school he ran away from home, determined to become a riverboat pilot, a dream he had cherished all his school life.

But it was to be many years before he was to achieve that ambition. For he began his working life as a printer's apprentice and worked on his brother's newspaper the Hannibal *Journal*. It was a fairly uneventful start to a life which was to be packed with excitement. He began to travel the country, working his way eastwards on newspapers in St. Louis, New York and Philadelphia. But even this wandering, carefree life was not enough to satisfy the restless, impatient spirit which stirred the imagination of the young American journalist.

Wildly infected with a fever for exotic places, and the adventure he would find there, Clemens found himself in 1856, starting down the Mississippi on a trip he had planned to the Amazon. But childhood ambitions had still not been fulfilled and he ended up as an apprentice to a riverboat pilot.

After eighteen months learning the strange mysteries of navigating the tortuous channels of the Mississippi, Clemens obtained a pilot's licence. His boyhood dream had become a reality.

This was the boom period of the steamboat and Clemens enjoyed almost every moment of his six years on the river. Then, in 1861, the American Civil War disrupted the river traffic, and Clemens spent a few inglorious weeks as a Confederate soldier before he decided to leave the army and search elsewhere for fun and adventure. He set off to find his fortune digging for silver in Nevada. Clemens found there, not wealth, but a mass of material which he was later to use as a writer. For he learned not only the hardships of a silver prospector's life, but also much about the behaviour of human beings.

For more than a week he found himself trapped inside a lonely Nevada inn before he decided to defy the fierce blizzards and floods which were sweeping across the countryside. He set out with a Prussian officer and a miner, and within minutes, their canoe was being swept along by a raging current. The officer jumped overboard in a fit of panic, and the canoe overturned. Clemens narrowly escaped death only to find himself facing it again the next day. The following morning they set off again. This time by horse. But the road was completely hidden by snow, and the three men wandered helplessly amongst the sage bush which led into the heart of the desert.

"Plainly", recorded Clemens later, "after this the situation was desperate. We were cold and stiff, and the horses were tired." When they had lost all hope of survival, the storm abated, and they found that they were only a few yards from a wooden stagecoach station! Once again, Samuel Clemens had lived through an adventure which was to help him write such lively, exciting tales when he became Mark Twain, the writer.

He had certainly lived through some hair-raising experiences, but his life as a silver prospector was over. He had started off with a buoyant enthusiasm and with dreams of gaining immense riches, but in the end, the harsh punishment of the living conditions and the dangers involved forced him to give it up. He hated to give in, and it was only with a certain amount of reluctance that he returned to journalism.

Four years later, the charm of distant places lured him once again. This time his travels took him to the Hawaiian Islands, to France, Italy, Greece, Turkey and the Holy Land. The result led to the publication of *Innocents Abroad*, Twain's first really successful work.

He had adopted the pen name Mark Twain which is riverboat jargon for two fathoms deep, and it is by this name that he is known throughout the world. *Innocents Abroad* was an instant success. His sharply observed descriptions of foreign places were greatly admired but above all, it was the humour which bounced off every page, that delighted its readers.

It was Twain's wonderful sense of humour which gave *The Adventures of Tom Sawyer*, and *Huckleberry Finn* such world-wide appeal. Tom, though not 'the model boy of the village', is goodhearted and full of fun. Again and again, this irresponsible, naughty boy triumphs over 'goody-goodies' who, unlike Tom, are ever-ready to tell tales and get other people into scrapes. The town of St. Petersburg of the novel, is really Hannibal, and many of the people portrayed in it, are characters which Mark Twain knew as a young boy.

Then, with *Huckleberry Finn*, Twain achieves his greatest triumph. An outstanding novel by any standards, it features the character of Huck, son of the village drunkard, whose compassion, tolerance and shrewdness shine out above all his faults. He runs away with a slave called Jim, and the story of their adventures down the Mississippi on a raft make up the theme of the novel.

In these and his other books, *Life On The Mississippi*, *A Connecticut Yankee At The Court Of King Arthur*, and *Roughing It*, Twain used a style which was distinctly his own. For the first time an American writer had offered a style that was completely American, not merely a poor European imitation. His works are an unusual combination of vivid imagination, delightful humour, and shrewd common sense in his understanding of human behaviour.

Happily, he was to enjoy all the fame and success as a writer in his own lifetime. And just as Mark Twain comes across to us as a witty, wise and fascinating writer, so it was with Samuel Clemens, the man. For he never lost his restless, impatient spirit, and although his mind grew up, he remained at heart, a boy.

He found it difficult to lead a quiet life and although he probably wanted to belong to respectable, fashionable society, his sense of humour could never allow him to take that society very seriously. He often outraged acquaintances with his scandalous remarks, uttered, more often than not, simply to shock them.

But the seventy-five years of his life were not all fun and happiness. Despite the personal tragedies which tormented him (the deaths of his wife, son, and two daughters), he lived life to the full. Even by the time he had settled down to become an author in 1871 at the age of thirty six, he had packed enough excitement and adventure into his life, to write a hundred and one books from his experiences.

Battling against the blinding blizzard, the three men and their horses wandered helplessly among the sage bush.

47

OUR WONDERFUL WORLD OF ARTS QUIZ

See how much you have learned from reading the articles in the Arts section of this book by trying to answer these questions :

1. No one knows for sure when coloured glass was first used for windows, but the oldest examples date from A.D.1,000. Where are these windows?

2. The Last Judgement Window was placed in the most important part of the church. What other name was given to this type of window?

3. Who composed the opera, 'The Flying Dutchman'?

4. Who rises up to heaven at the end of this opera?

5. Was Frankenstein the name of a fictional monster or the scientist who is supposed to have created it?

6. Who wrote the original story of Frankenstein? When and where did the author get the idea of this story?

7. Who was the actor who played the part of the monster in the first film version of the story in 1931?

8. Two cartoon film series featured the monster. Can you give the titles of these?

9. What does the term Watercolour mean?

10. Who founded the English Watercolour school?

11. Where was the artist, J. M. W. Turner born, and what was his father's occupation?

12. If you rolled some dried peas or lead shot in a hatbox or on top of a drum or sieve, what sound effect would you produce?

13. For the sound of horses' hooves on a hard surface, what would you use?

14. Who wrote the 'Destruction of Sennacherib'?

15. Who was Sennacherib?

16. What was Mark Twain's real name.

17. What is the name of the town in which he grew up and which he used as a background for some of his books?

18. Name the river which flowed by his town, and which is a great trade route across America.

19. What was Mark Twain's boyhood ambition?

20. Twain's travels to Europe, Hawaii and the Holy Land resulted in the publication of his first really successful work. What was this book called?

THE ANSWERS ARE AT THE BACK OF THE BOOK.

CHALLENGE OF THE OCEAN DEPTHS

Ever since man made his first dug-out canoe from a tree trunk, and cautiously floated it a few yards from the shore, he has been fascinated by the sea.

Nobody really knows when man began to explore the oceans, but it is reasonable to suppose that if he lived near the coasts of the great continents, he would have made some attempt to find out more about the apparently limitless expanse of ocean that met his eyes.

Prehistoric man's life must have been a constant struggle for survival dominated by an endless search for food, and the sea was an obvious place to look.

We know from archaeological evidence that part of our early ancestors' diet consisted of fish. Skeletons of fish have been discovered in settlements

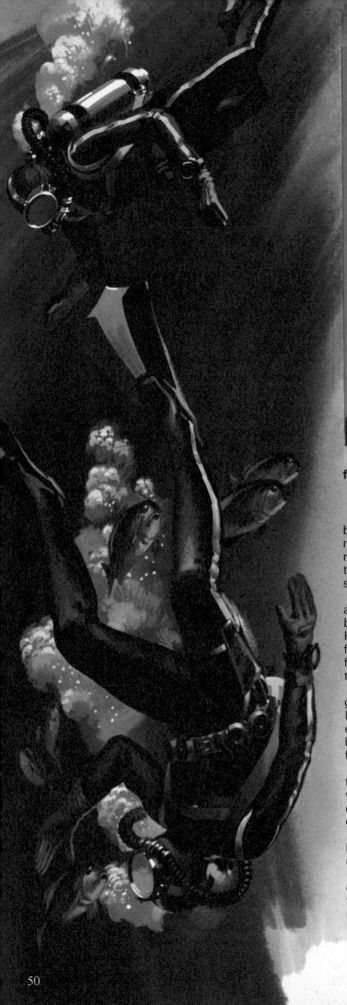

When a diver goes too deep and stays down for too long, he suffers from what the famous French undersea explorer Jacques Cousteau (above) called 'Rapture of the Deep'.

bordering the sea. We know, too, that Paleolithic man used wooden harpoons to spear fish among the rocks and shallows, and it is more than likely that in time he would have become bolder and learned to swim and dive in his search for additional food.

As centuries rolled by, man gradually learned more and more about the oceans. He learned how to build bigger and more reliable ships, and how to navigate. He also became much more skilled in the art of fishing until, in modern times, the amount of food from the sea made a significant contribution to the total world supply.

One thing, however, the mighty sea refused to give up easily—and that was the secret of its depths. For centuries men were frustrated in their efforts to explore even the shallower parts of the ocean floor because of their inability to survive for more than a few minutes under the surface.

The first men to dive to any depth were, of course, the early sponge divers who earned their living in the warmer seas of the world by descending to depths of between 50 to 100 feet with no diving equipment other than a large stone to carry them down.

Apart from sponges, these 'aquanauts' also brought various sea shells to the surface which were used as household utensils, and ornaments.

Although some attempt was made to supply divers with air somewhere around 300 BC by sending them down in crudely made diving bells, many centuries were to pass before men fully realised they had one great problem to overcome before anyone could stay beneath the surface of the sea for long periods. It is the problem of *pressure*.

The deeper a man dives the greater is the pressure on his body exerted by the water around him. This does not mean that you would be squashed flat at great depth. Most of the human body is made up of incompressible fluids, bone and tissue, and the pressure of the water is distributed evenly from every direction. It therefore has little effect on the body as a whole, but it does have an effect on any hollow cavities such as the middle ear, and the lungs.

If, however, these cavities can have the pressure equalised by a supply of air, then the diver can survive. But that is not the end of the problem—it is really only the beginning, and it took doctors and scientists many years to understand why divers became ill, and even died, when they returned to the surface after spending some time at depths of 200 feet or more.

The atmosphere we all breathe at sea level consists roughly of 21 per cent oxygen, 79 per cent nitrogen and a trace of carbon dioxide. As we take a breath the delicate membranes in our lungs absorb into the bloodstream about one quarter of the oxygen and as we breath out we get rid of the other three quarters together with all the nitrogen (none of which is absorbed), and most of the carbon dioxide.

Something quite different happens, however, when air is breathed under pressure. Then, the body begins to absorb the nitrogen into the bloodstream, and the deeper a diver goes, and the longer he stays underwater, the more of this unwanted gas gets into his body.

The effects of this are two-fold. At depths of about 50 fathoms (300 feet, one fathom = 6 feet) so much nitrogen is absorbed that it begins to affect the brain. The diver suffers from what the famous French undersea explorer Jacques Cousteau named 'Rapture of the Deep', and feels unusually happy and confident. He may even feel that he really is a fish and can swim deeper and deeper. Of course, he cannot, and eventually he would lose consciousness and drown.

The other effect is known as the 'bends', a name which comes from the symptoms shown by any unlucky diver who comes to the surface too quickly, and who suffers pains in his joints which make him contort and bend about to try to obtain relief.

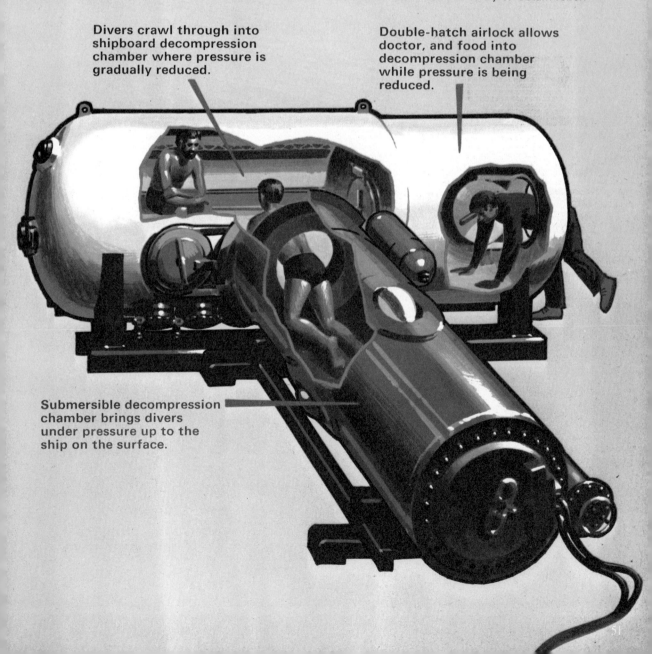

Divers crawl through into shipboard decompression chamber where pressure is gradually reduced.

Double-hatch airlock allows doctor, and food into decompression chamber while pressure is being reduced.

Submersible decompression chamber brings divers under pressure up to the ship on the surface.

The reason for the 'bends' is that as a diver rises to the surface and the pressure gradually decreases, the nitrogen in his blood begins to bubble off in his veins and arteries. He can be compared with a soda-water syphon, the contents of which will bubble when the valve is opened.

The 'bends' can be avoided either by bringing the diver up in stages and leaving him hanging by his lifeline at various depths so that his body can gradually rid itself of the poisonous nitrogen, or by placing him straight into a decompression chamber.

In the decompression chamber various depths can be simulated by using compressed air, and the diver can slowly be brought back to normal atmospheric pressure without the discomfort of dangling for long periods in cold sea water.

Modern technology is slowly overcoming the immense problems connected with man's ever widening exploration of 'the land beneath the sea'. Giant nuclear-powered submarines, although now only used for defence purposes, will ultimately be adapted as cargo carrying vessels.

Smaller submarines known as submersibles already exist, and are capable of descending to immense depths, and many other specially designed deep-sea craft are coming along.

Like our prehistoric ancestors who were driven by necessity to search the sea for food, we too will of necessity have to extract not only food, but also raw materials from the sea bed. Undersea farming, and undersea mining will become commonplace in the 21st century, and it is almost certain that we shall see undersea towns in which aquanauts will live and work.

But will men ever be able to live like the fishes in this alien environment? This is most unlikely because of the difficulties of changing or adapting our physical make-up. Even if it were possible surgically to change a man's lungs so that they could extract oxygen from water instead of air, he would still find most of the oceans of the world too cold to survive in them for very long.

Giant underwater oil tankers are a possibility for the future. They could be loaded with crude oil from an ocean floor oil refinery, while submerged, thus avoiding any bad weather problems on the surface.

Two American submersibles named *Alvin* and *Aluminaut* were the first of the new generation of deep sea diving vessels to be used in man's exploration of the ocean bed.

Alvin and *Aluminaut* were used in 1966 to recover a nuclear bomb which accidentally fell from an aircraft into 2,500 feet of water in the Mediterranean. The finding and raising of the bomb was a remarkable example of the uses to which this type of vessel can be put.

The *Aluminaut* is a fairly large submersible and can sustain a three-man crew for up to three days. It is built mainly of 6½ inch thick aluminium, hence its name, and can cruise at a depth of three miles.

Alvin is much smaller—22 feet in length—and its steel sphere can withstand the pressure of the sea at depths of over 6,000 feet.

Great Britain, too, is well ahead with its underwater exploration vehicles, and is probably the only country in Europe operating these deep ocean vessels on a working commercial basis.

The company which has done so much to put Britain in the forefront is Vickers Shipbuilding Group who formed a department in 1966 known as Vickers Oceanics.

After years of experimenting and developing underwater vessels, the company now operates on a fully commercial basis providing services to offshore oil rigs, deep sea cable laying companies, etc.

Support ships are needed from which the submersibles can operate. Vickers Oceanics have two of these—the *Vickers Venturer*, an ex-stern trawler of 630 tons, and the much larger *Vickers Voyager* depicted on this page.

The *Vickers Voyager* is a well equipped vessel

Above: The *Vickers Voyager* support ship which acts as a mother ship to the *Pisces* submersibles. This vessel took part in the dramatic rescue of a two-man submersible off the coast of Ireland in 1973.

which has been extensively re-fitted. Originally built as a fish-factory ship it has a displacement tonnage of 4,500 tons, an overall length of 274 feet 8 inches and a beam of 48 feet.

Two submersibles named *Pisces* (described in detail on page 56) are carried in the stern of the ship in a special hangar. They can be launched singly by means of specially developed handling equipment (see picture on right).

One of the problems of launching any kind of small vessel from a larger one is the movement of the sea. Even a lifeboat is difficult to launch from ship in rough seas, but Vickers have designed what is known as an 'A' Frame (because of its shape) which swings the submersible out from the stern of the support ship and lowers it into the sea.

The little submersibles are recovered in the same way. A wave-compensating winch which keeps the hoisting rope taut enables both launching and recovery to take place in seas with waves up to 14 feet high.

Voyager is fitted with large workshops in which the submersibles can be repaired and maintained. The ship also carries a decompression chamber for ordinary divers who may be needed in salvage work.

Navigation equipment in the *Voyager* includes a satellite navigation system with which the ship can pin-point its position using the fixed position space satellites above the earth. Sonar underwater listening

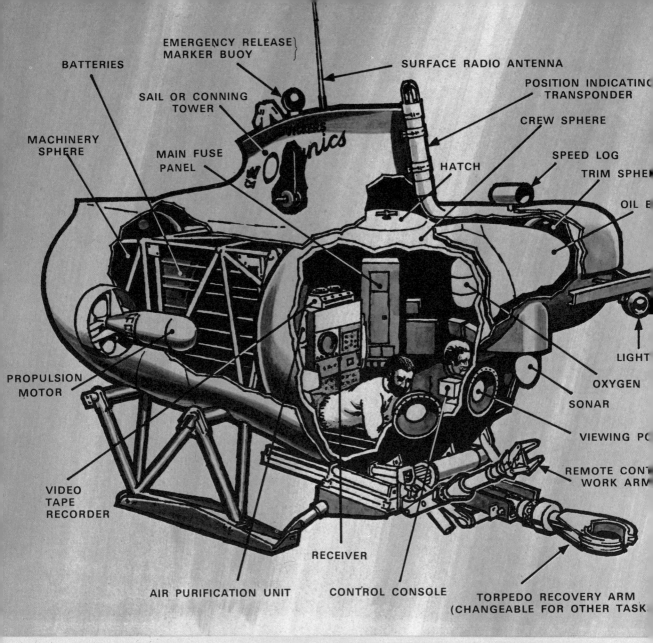

BATTERIES

EMERGENCY RELEASE MARKER BUOY

SAIL OR CONNING TOWER

SURFACE RADIO ANTENNA

POSITION INDICATING TRANSPONDER

CREW SPHERE

MACHINERY SPHERE

MAIN FUSE PANEL

HATCH

SPEED LOG

TRIM SPHER

OIL B

LIGHT

OXYGEN

SONAR

VIEWING PC

PROPULSION MOTOR

REMOTE CONT WORK ARM

VIDEO TAPE RECORDER

RECEIVER

AIR PURIFICATION UNIT

CONTROL CONSOLE

TORPEDO RECOVERY ARM (CHANGEABLE FOR OTHER TASK

gear is also carried, and an underwater tracking system known as SPATE (Submersible Position and Tracking Equipment) is fitted.

Voyager is also fully air-conditioned so that it can be operated in both tropical and temperate areas of the world, and has accommodation for 20 passengers in addition to its crew. Its top speed is 12½ knots.

The *Pisces* submersible was designed originally in Canada and modifications and improvements were made by Vickers in Britain. Its basic construction consists of two steel spheres. The crew sphere, which is 6 feet 8 inches in diameter, is capable of withstanding the pressure of the sea down to a depth of 3,600 feet. A later model, made in this country, can descend to 6,000 feet.

The crew sphere has three viewing ports which give the two-man crew a 180° field of vision. The second sphere aft contains machinery. Two 3 hp electric motors placed like 'ears' on each side of the hull provide the motive power. Electricity is provided by a large capacity lead-acid battery, and the vessel can travel at speeds up to 4 knots while submerged.

A great deal of equipment is carried inside the

crew compartment, including such things as a depth sounder, an indicator directional gyro, a depth gauge, a closed circuit TV system connected to a video tape recorder, sonar and radio, and a transponder for tracking and guidance by the mother ship.

Work carried out underwater is done mainly by a large hydraulically operated 'torpedo' grab and a general purpose manipulator, both of which are operated by the crew. Other tools can be added such as a drill, an impact wrench and a mud pump. Tools can be interchanged while the vessel is submerged.

The *Pisces*' life support systems are sufficient to allow its crew to remain submerged for up to 72 hours. Safety equipment incorporated includes an alarm which sounds when the air inside the sphere contains too much carbon dioxide, and another which warns of any water leaks.

If the submersible gets stuck on the bottom of the ocean and cannot raise itself by blowing the ballast tanks, the crew can jettison the 'claw', the manipulator, the motors and a drop weight to increase buoyancy.

Here you see an operator loading glass-making materials into a tank. From there, they are fed into the furnace where the great heat fuses them together and makes the glass.

RIVERS OF GLASS

If you have ever accidentally tried to walk through a closed glass door, you will know that there's more to glass than meets the eye!

Glass is one of those substances which, like precious metals and gemstones, perpetually fascinate mankind. Objects which gleam or glitter will always attract attention. Glass has an attraction beyond even that of gold or silver, for light can pass entirely through it. It is transparent and yet solid. Or so it appears.

In actual fact, glass is not a solid. It is a liquid.

There is no danger of window-panes suddenly running down the walls, like treacle. Windows struck by footballs will still shatter, not splash. Glass in a window pane flows so slowly that no movement is ever likely to be detected by ordinary vision. Calculations show that thousands of millions of years would pass before the flow became noticeable under ordinary temperatures and conditions. Yet this slowly-flowing liquid is, in theory, many times stronger than the finest steel.

Ordinary glass, of course, cannot support greater loads than those borne by steel. Because it is a liquid, it is very easily affected by any strains placed upon the

tiny cracks or other flaws in its surface. Think of a stone thrown into water. Ripples spread swiftly and evenly outwards from the splash, for there is nothing to stop them. Water is *homogeneous*—it has the same nature wherever the stone strikes it. There are no gaps, hard lumps or other 'discontinuities' to break the movement of the ripples. Similarly, in glass, there are no discontinuities to stop the spreading of a crack, and so a glass object can disintegrate at great speed.

A lot of the work which has gone into developing different types of glass has been directed towards overcoming this weakness. No-one has yet succeeded in equalling the legendary feat of a craftsman of Ancient Rome, who supposedly produced a goblet which merely flattened when it was dropped, and could be beaten back into shape, but the Romans

After sheet glass comes from the furnace, it travels slowly up a thirty foot tower. On its way, it gradually cools and in this picture it has reached the top of the tower and is ready to be removed.

The grinding is carried out by twin grinders like these. The surfaces are made parallel and this gives the plate glass its extreme clarity and lack of distortion.

Photographs by courtesy of Pilkington Bros. Ltd.

would regard many modern achievements as being equally incredible.

Typical of the problems faced by today's workers in glass is that of providing cockpit canopies for supersonic aircraft such as the Concorde. High in the thin air, these machines are exposed to extremes of heat and cold, and because they are above the denser layers of the atmosphere which absorb much of the barrage of radiation from the sun and outer space, they receive a larger share of cosmic rays and ultra-violet.

＊＊＊＊

Canopies must shield the aircrew against these hazards, and at the same time give them a clear field of view. Lamination, the building up of a sandwich made of several layers of toughened glass, is part of the answer. On the inner side of this sandwich, a layer of gold thin enough to be transparent will conduct an electric current which generates sufficient heat to prevent icing-up. And in the passenger section of the aircraft, glass fibre insulation muffles the roar of the jet engines and keeps out the savage cold.

On the ground, under the protection of a miles-deep 'roof' of air and water-vapour, there is still enough sunlight and other radiation filtering through to keep scientists busy. As civilization consumes increasing amounts of energy, many foresee a time when coal and oil supplies will be exhausted. Because nuclear power creates dangerously radioactive waste, scientists seek a clean energy source, and an obvious choice is sunlight.

We receive more energy from the sun on one average day than humanity could use in forty years, but to be usable it must be concentrated and stored. Researchers in Arizona, USA, have constructed a mirror from a type of glass which absorbs sunlight and traps the infra-red, or heat, portion. This trapped heat operates a boiler which powers a steam-driven generator, which in turn produces electricity. Since infra-red rays can penetrate clouds, the mirror functions even when the sun is hidden.

This device could be described as a heat telescope. In ordinary telescopes, the accuracy of the lens is of great importance, and the larger the lens the more difficult it is to manufacture.

A curious fact about the use of glass in the mirrors of giant *reflecting* telescopes such as that at California's Mount Palomar observatory, is that it serves no optical purpose. Normally, the metallic light-reflecting layer of a mirror is behind the glass, but in these instruments the layer is laid over the glass, which is thus cut off from the light. It is the other properties of glass which cause it to be chosen for this job. The high degree of accuracy with which it can be smoothed and shaped, its resistance to the distorting effects of heat, and the way in which it combines lightness and strength.

Without this versatile substance, the science of astronomy as we know it today could never have existed, and the visible Universe would be limited to what keen eyes and clear skies could reveal.

Despite the long history of manufactured glass, stretching back at least 5,000 years, scientists have only recently begun to understand its true nature. As a result, its uses have increased enormously during this century, and its future possibilities seem limitless.

From factories around the world, bottles, bulbs and tubes pour out in a river of glass. A single machine can produce 9,000 bottles hourly; another can turn out 1,000 light-bulbs per minute,

A ribbon of molten glass 100 feet wide is being drawn from the end of a machine making plate glass of the kind used in shop windows.

The long ribbon of plate glass has now been removed and the next stage is the important grinding and polishing.

ready for sealing. Corrosive chemicals and baby foods, soft drinks and shampoos, all have their appropriate type of glass container.

Among many new techniques being devised in laboratories, the transmission of pictures via optical glass fibres is one of the most exciting. Cartoonists have often used the notion of a telescope which could see around corners, as a subject for humour. Fibre optics have made it possible.

Glass is drawn out into long, extremely fine threads, or fibres, which are laid side by side in a bundle. The bundle is then cut to whatever length is required, and the tips at each end are sealed together. These ends are then polished as if each was a solid lens. The result looks rather like a doctor's stethoscope minus the middle 'leg'. If one end was held above the words you are reading now, they would be visible at the other end, the image being transmitted through the fibres. This would happen even if the bundle was twisted into a circle, or bent around a corner. And pictures are only the beginning. When experiments being carried out at Southampton University and else-

where are developed on a commercial scale, telephone messages will be carried by breaking down the sound waves into pulses of light. Such a system should be capable of carrying many thousand times more messages than the present telephone links.

We still have some distance to go, however, before we catch up with the way Nature uses glass. Studying the fossil remains of trilobites, those shelled and many-legged creatures which were once the highest form of life in the oceans, an American researcher has discovered that they had eyes of crystal. The fossilized trilobites died 450 million years ago.

SOUND WAVES ON STAMPS

There is a close link between radio and the postal service, and many stamps have paid tribute to radio and TV. By C. W. Hill

In the autumn of 1894 a young Italian conducted a remarkable experiment in the garden of his home near Bologna. He asked his father to stand beside a piece of apparatus erected on the lawn. Then, from inside the house, he made the apparatus tap out the three dots of the Morse Code letter S.

Seven years later the same Italian sat on a hill in Newfoundland and heard the same letter transmitted to him across the Atlantic from Poldhu, in Cornwall.

By then the name of Marconi was becoming known as the pioneer of 'wire-less telegraphy', the science of telegraphing messages without using wires. But radio, as it is now called, was not the invention of one man. Like its later development, television, it resulted from the accumulated work of scientists from several countries who made electricity and electro-magnetism accessible to mankind.

There is a close link between radio and the postal services, since both are used for communication, so it is not surprising that many postage stamps have paid tribute to radio and television. An interesting collection illustrating this theme can be formed easily and cheaply.

The electro-magnetic waves which are the basis of radio, television and radar were discovered by Heinrich Hertz (1857-1894), a German engineer whose portrait has appeared on stamps from West Germany, Czechoslovakia and Monaco. Guglielmo Marconi (1874-1937), who came to Britain to continue his researches, is portrayed on stamps from Italy and Czechoslovakia.

While Marconi was making his early experiments, a Russian professor named Alexander Popov (1859-1905) was also experimenting independently in electricity and radio. Popov is now generally acknowledged to have been the first to transmit a radio signal, although his work was neither as successful nor as well publicised as Marconi's spectacular achievements. Popov has been honoured by several Russian portrait stamps and by issues from Bulgaria, Czechoslovakia and Hungary.

Stamp designers have often used radio waves to symbolise the speed of modern telecommunications. Waves radiating from a human eye across the starry heavens formed the design of the first issue in honour of television. It was a 40-centimes stamp in a series from Switzerland marking the centenary of the Swiss telegraph service.

Other designs have featured the television screen, and an unusual 10-pfennigs stamp issued in 1957 in West Germany showed the pattern of light seen when the set is first switched on. The inauguration of television services in Italy in 1954, in Czechoslovakia in 1957 and in Hungary in 1958 was commemorated in those countries by special stamps.

Also popular as a symbol of telecommunications are the tall masts of transmitting stations. The most celebrated of these, the Eiffel Tower, in Paris, has been shown on a French 15-francs stamp and on a 1-riyal stamp from the Arabian oil state of Dubai.

As well as many stamps featuring radio receivers, microphones and television screens, there are hundreds of issues showing the exploration of the Moon, an achievement which would have been impossible without radio and television.

1. Czechoslovakia, 60-heller: **Guglielmo Marconi**
2. West Germany, 10-pfennigs: **Heinrich Hertz**
3. Bulgaria, 90-stotinki: **Alexander Popov**
4. Switzerland, 40-centimes: **television**
5. Italy, 60-lire: inauguration of **television service**
6. West Germany, 10-pfennigs: **television screen**
7. Czechoslovakia, 40-heller: **transmitter**
8. Czechoslovakia, 60-heller: **television programme**
9. France, 15-francs: **Eiffel Tower**
10. Monaco, 50-centimes: **Television Festival, 1965**
11. Dubai, 5-riyals: **Eiffel Tower and Goonhilly aerial**
12. Egypt, 10-mills: **Electronic Exhibition, 1953**
13. Egypt, 10-mills: **Television Festival, 1963**
14. Great Britain, 3p: **microphones**
15. Great Britain, 7½p: **television camera**
16. East Germany, 20-pfennigs: **television screen**
17. China, 8-fen: **wild goose and radio pylon**
18. Austria, 1-schilling: **radio receiver**
19. Liberia, 50-cents: **International Telecommunications Union**
20. Ras al Khaima, 1-riyal: **Apollo XV Moon mission**

INTO SPACE WITH WINGS

A white hot ball of fire streaks through the sky towards Earth from the far distances of outer space. Gradually it cools and lands like an aeroplane ready to be used for another journey to the planets. A vision of the future? Perhaps, but one that could be a practical possibility, as this article shows.

EVERYONE knows what a space shot looks like. The huge rocket, shaped something like a church spire and at least as big, blasts thunderously towards the sky. Perched on top is the payload, which is relatively very small. Hardly anything comes back to Earth. The great rocket is used only once, even though it costs millions of dollars.

Think how impossibly costly life would be if cars, planes, ships and trains were all used just once and then thrown away! To try to bring down the cost of space travel, NASA (the US National Aeronautics and Space Administration) has decided in future to try to use giant space vehicles again and again.

Eight years ago NASA scientists and engineers began to work on the Space Shuttle, a huge launch vehicle that may be used as many as 100 times. Though the Shuttle will cost much more than earlier space rockets, it is hoped to reduce the expense of space exploration very considerably.

✳ ✳ ✳ ✳

Originally it was thought it could reduce space-flight costs to only 1/30th as much as using "once-only" rockets. Even though the Shuttle has—like so many other things—been badly hit by soaring prices, it is still hoped to fly each space mission much more cheaply than has been possible hitherto.

Before launch, a Shuttle looks rather like three big rockets clustered tightly together carrying a kind of aeroplane on the side, pointing nose-upwards. In fact the "aeroplane" is really an "aerospace plane", because it can fly equally well in the Earth's atmosphere or in outer space. It is called the Orbiter, because it is the part of the Shuttle that goes into orbit and carries the payload of cargo or passengers. People have been drawing pictures of such things for years, but nothing like it has been built before.

The first Orbiter, now being built in the United States, will be 126 feet long, or about the same as a medium-sized jetliner. It will have a rather stumpy shape and a very tall fin (as tall as a seven-storey building). Some Orbiters will have ordinary aeroplane jet engines, to help them fly like other aircraft before landing back at their Earth airfield, but these will only be used in the last few minutes of each flight.

✳ ✳ ✳ ✳

The main engines are powerful rockets, giving a total push of almost 600 tons. These engines will be different from those used in earlier space missions in that they will be designed to last for as many as 100 flights, and they will be controlled by the pilot who will be able to move throttle levers to change the rocket power, just as he can control the power of ordinary aircraft engines.

These main engines will run on the same mixture as was used to send men to the Moon: liquid oxygen and liquid hydrogen, both of them cooled to such an extremely low temperature that the gas turns into a liquid. Some of the liquid oxygen and liquid hydrogen will be carried in the Orbiter, but most of it will be stored in a huge insulated tank which is by far the biggest single part of the whole craft. It will be well over 180 feet high and 26 feet in diameter. There could be ample room inside for seven underground trains side by side! When filled it will weigh more than 700 tons, and it will feed its vital liquids to the Orbiter

What could become a space vehicle of the future is the British designed craft shown here which is made up of three units, all of which return to Earth. See page 66 for more details.

65

through large pipe couplings.

On each side of this huge tank will be strapped an SRM (solid rocket motor). Rockets do not, of course, have to run on liquids. Each SRM will be filled with solid fuel and, like the simple Guy Fawkes kind, lit at the bottom before take-off. Unlike the Guy Fawkes rocket each SRM will have a casing of very strong steel, weighing altogether 1,600 tons! When both SRMs are firing they will each give a push of almost 2,000 tons, so that the total thrust sending the flight on its way will be 9,515,000 pounds or about 4,300 tons! This is the biggest push ever given to any flying vehicle. It's a good thing that nobody will have to light any blue touch-paper, though the fact that the Shuttle will carry people means its safety will have to be very good indeed.

✳ ✳ ✳ ✳

This push of 4,300 tons will send the Shuttle skywards even faster than earlier space rockets. The pilot will be able to steer by using special controls that deflect the directions of the big rocket engines. About 40 seconds from launch the thrust of the big SRMs will be reduced, to stop the acceleration from getting uncomfortably high (because as the fuel is burned the whole Shuttle gets lighter, so the acceleration would keep on getting greater).

At a height of some 25 miles the SRMs will burn out, drop off, parachute into the sea and then be recovered and towed ashore for overhaul, refilling and re-use up to a maximum of ten times. The Orbiter will carry on into an easterly orbit round the Earth at a height of 115 miles. Then the empty tank will be cast off and allowed to fall back to Earth and burn up (it will not cost a great deal, in comparison with the rest of the Shuttle). The Orbiter will then continue with its mission.

It may have to climb, dive, change its orbit, dock with a space station or do many other things. On the back of the Orbiter is a big cargo bay, about 15 feet across and 65 feet long, in which can be carried passengers, laboratories, spacecraft and other items, as well as a "space tug" (a self-contained rocket vehicle) which can be coupled up to carry loads farther away from Earth.

✳ ✳ ✳ ✳

The list of missions for the Shuttle is literally endless, because fresh tasks are arising all the time. It includes inspection and surveys of traffic in space, aircraft traffic survey and control, shipping and ground traffic and communication monitoring, geographical surveys and mapping, weather studies and forecasts, assessment and management of all the Earth's resources—agriculture, forestry, minerals, oceans, water and fisheries—and warning and minute-by-minute watch over all major hazards such as forest fires, floods and eathquakes.

The Shuttle will also have to fulfil many missions dealing with the establishment and maintenance of communication satellites, used all over the world for

Multi-Unit Space Transport and Recovery Device (Mustard) is the name of this craft designed in Britain. Here is how it works. 1. After the unit has blasted off with all motors firing, the outer units break away in the upper atmosphere. 2. The centre unit goes into orbit with its payload. 3. The unit re-enters the Earth's atmosphere. 4. It lands on a normal aircraft runway. Meanwhile, the outer units have also returned to base.

Above right: another type of space transporter designed to return to Earth after going into orbit

telephone and TV services and to bring educational and other broadcasts to remote people who have no local radio or TV station. On each mission a Shuttle may carry many different kinds of payload, each part assigned to a particular kind of duty. Thus there may be astronauts to be taken to a space station, a repair crew with spare parts to be taken to repair a satellite, and there may be a complete spacecraft to be delivered by space tug somewhere else.

* * * *

At the end of its mission, loaded up with fresh passengers and cargo, the Shuttle will re-start its engines for Earth. It will be thermally protected by special coatings against the white-hot searing heat of re-entry as it falls back into the atmosphere. The pilot will have to keep it pointing exactly in the right direction during this crucial phase, by firing special small rocket engines arranged at the extremities of the body and wings to tilt it back to the correct attitude.

When the re-entry is complete the shuttle Orbiter will be flying at a much reduced speed inside the atmosphere, supported on its broad wing and guided by ordinary control surfaces such as are used on aircraft. It will be able to fly like this for up to 1,100 miles, steering for its home base. Finally it will come in to land at about 175 mph on its destination runway —a far better way to arrive than plopping into the ocean sealed in a capsule, which must then be lifted by a helicopter!

Nobody quite knows how many times the various bits of the space Shuttle will be used. Perhaps some will be damaged or lost, while other parts that are recovered may later fail some test that will prevent them from being re-used. But it is hoped that the SRMs will be used up to ten times, and that the expensive Orbiter will last as many as 100 missions.

The Orbiter is likely to fly as an aircraft in 1976, and the complete Shuttle is scheduled to go into use in the United States in 1982. NASA expects to keep a fleet of between five and eight constantly in use, operating from Cape Kennedy in Florida and Vandenberg in California. They may fly about 50 or 60 missions every year. Soon space travel will be no more a problem than hopping on a bus!

MAN NEEDS MORE ENERGY

Primitive man had no source of energy but his own muscles, and those of domesticated animals. Then he learned to harness the wind to drive sailing ships and windmills, and the water of rivers to drive water-wheels.

Modern man has a fantastic wealth of energy sources. Some of these are what are called "fossil" sources, because they are stored in the ground in the form of fossil material, such as coal or petroleum. Others include the burning of wood, peat or other combustible material, the extraction of heat from nuclear fuels such as uranium, and using the heat from the Sun. Not only do we have many kinds of energy at our command, but we can also send it where it is wanted and use it whenever we choose. The way we do this is by converting the energy into electricity, which can then be used for countless purposes.

Altogether the story of man's search for more and better sources of energy is one of brilliant success. Instead of having a lifetime of back-breaking toil he has made other sorts of energy do the work for him, to keep him cool in summer, warm in winter, carry him from place to place, and generally make life easier.

But really man's supplies of energy are a cause for deep concern. This is because man is using up Earth's supplies of energy faster and faster, yet he is doing little or nothing to replace the supplies, and there is a risk that most of the present sources will one day be exhausted. As we are not

Each year the world is using up more and more of its natural energy resources. As the situation grows more serious scientists are seeking to find alternative means of power . . .

likely to enjoy going back to sleeping in cold caves and doing everything with our muscles, there can be seen to be a big problem. How can we solve it?

First we must take a closer look at the different sorts of energy. One of the most basic forms of energy is heat. Obviously we release heat when we burn something, but it is easy to forget that our bodies also extract heat from our food. We measure the energy we get from food in "calories", and these are a measure of heat.

Most of man's food sources are self-replenishing. Crops, fish and edible animals keep on reproducing themselves. Though all man's food systems depend upon sunlight as their ultimate source of energy, the fact that fresh food is growing all the time means that there is no immediate danger of food supplies running out (except in temporary local famines which, though terrible for the people affected, do not touch mankind as a whole).

Man's other energy supplies are unable to reproduce themselves. Coal, oil and other fossil fuels took about 250 million years to form, and though fresh coal and petroleum is forming in many parts of the Earth it is doing so very slowly indeed. So when coal, oil or natural gas has been taken from the Earth it is a one-way process. Nothing is put back.

What happens when these vital fuels are burned? They are made mostly of hydrogen and carbon, and these elements combine with the oxygen of the atmosphere to make new compounds such as water vapour, carbon dioxide and small quantities of nitrogen and sulphur. There is no way of catching these "products of combustion" and turning them back into fresh fuel, and even if it were attempted it would mean using up more energy to make the change.

What makes it worse is that these substances, which pour out of chimneys, exhaust pipes and everywhere else that fuel is burned, often cause smog, damage to buildings and disease to human lungs. Although most countries are making efforts to burn fuel more cleanly, it is impossible to stop pollution from this cause entirely. Man's demand for energy—which today means demand for fossil fuels—is increasing at a

frightening speed. What has kept everything going so far is that a frantic search for fresh supplies of oil and gas have allowed output to be stepped up to meet the demand. But, though the Earth is a big storehouse, the total amount of fossil fuel is strictly limited. What happens when none is left?

At present we have plenty of alternatives, but none that can provide more than a tiny fraction of man's energy needs. One obvious one is nuclear power. Nuclear fuels, such as uranium, thorium and plutonium, can be made to undergo "fission" in a controlled and steady way so that the material becomes extremely hot. When a cooling flow of gas or liquid is passed over the hot fuel this heat can be taken away and put to use.

Almost all today's nuclear power plants use this heat to drive big turbines to generate electricity, and as tomorrow's world will be almost all-electric this is very valuable. The main advantage of nuclear fuels is that they are used up very slowly. The heat that could be extracted from one ton of uranium is as much as that obtained by completely burning 3,000,000 tons of coal.

We cannot at present hope to have an all-nuclear world, because there are too many problems of cost, supplies of nuclear fuel, and disposal of the harmful radioactive "waste products" which are left behind when most types of nuclear fuel have been used. It is also difficult to make nuclear reactors small and light enough to be used in vehicles other than large ships.

Some countries have hydro-electric installations which use the energy of falling water to generate electricity. These are the modern equivalents of the water-wheel, and they have the great advantage that they use up none of the Earth's resources and leave no waste products. They are really just another way of using the Sun's heat, because it is this heat which lifts water molecules into the sky so that they can then fall again as rain, feeding the rivers which then pour in a torrent through the giant hydro-electric turbines.

These installations can only be built where there are both big rivers and steep descents, and in most countries hydro-power can provide only a very small fraction of the total

energy needed. Scientists have even wondered whether there might be a way of using the energy of the Earth's rotation. The amount of energy locked up in the spin of the Earth is huge; expressed in ergs—a unit used to measure energy—it would be 1,000,000,000,000,000,000,000,000,000,000,000,000! But so far nobody has found a way of using it. If they did, we should have a very good long-term supply of energy, at the cost of gradually slowing the Earth's spin so that days and nights became longer. Eventually the energy would all be used up, and the Earth would stop spinning on its axis and would bake on one side and freeze on the other! Perhaps it is just as well that man cannot yet bring this about.

An even bigger source of energy is the kinetic energy of the Earth's movement along its orbit around the Sun, but trying to use this would make the Earth come nearer and nearer to the Sun so that we should all be shrivelled up!

But how about using the Sun's heat directly? Already there are many small installations which do this. Some are tiny furnaces at the focal points of large mirrors, and others are special ponds which are made hot by the Sun's rays. But, unless engineers can discover how to make long-lasting mirrors many miles across, it is hard to see how solar energy can be used on a useful scale. On the other hand, there are indirect ways that look interesting. For example, hydro-electric power can harness only a small fraction of the Sun's

energy expended in raising the moisture into the sky. If huge reservoirs could be built miles above the ground to catch the rain as soon as it fell from the clouds, nearly all this energy might be recovered. But just try making a tank to hold millions of tons of water at the height of the clouds!

Most scientists think that man must one day find much better ways of using the Sun's heat. They also hope to perfect another way of using the vast energy locked up inside atoms by making them join together in a process called "fusion", which is almost the reverse of fission. Fusion makes the H-bomb work, but it has so far proved very difficult to control the process so that it can give power continuously.

Other scientists think the most important fuel early in the 21st century will be hydrogen, the most abundant element in the universe, which when refrigerated and stored as a liquid can be used in engines much as petrol and oils are used today. Burning hydrogen fuel merely produces water (which would just increase the rainfall a bit!) and electricity could then be used to split up the molecules of water back into oxygen and hydrogen for use all over again.

At present we cannot see very far ahead. All we can say for certain is that man's energy supplies of the mid-1970s, which are mainly fossil fuels taken from deep in the Earth, must be regarded as a purely temporary solution to the world-wide energy problem.

In the Western Pyrenees, French engineers have built this furnace which obtains a terrific heat from the rays of the sun. The sun's rays are reflected from mirrors on terraces on to the huge curved mirror which concentrates them into the mouth of a furnace which stands before it. Heat of up to 6,000 degrees Fahrenheit is created. This is put to industrial use.

The sun's heat is reflected by the rows of mirrors (A) mounted on the hillside. The mirrors are controlled from an overlooking room (B) in the rear of the furnace building. The reflected heat is concentrated into a narrow, accurate beam by the huge concave main mirror (C) and reflected on to the working area of the furnace (D). The furnace's operation is controlled from a room set in the face of the main mirror at a height level with the furnace. The main building (E) behind the big mirror houses research laboratories.

The microscope, one of the few pieces of equipment that is found in every type of biological laboratory, has revolutionised the science of unlocking the inner secrets of life.

STRANGE WORLD OF THE SUPER small

On your school ruler you probably have tenths of an inch marked. Look at a tenth of an inch for a moment and then try to imagine something less than one-hundredth the size of that small measurement.

That one-hundredth of a tenth—or thousandth of an inch—would be larger than the size of the largest bacteria known to man today.

Bacteria are everywhere, and they are both man's friend and his enemy.

Today, we know that they are far more complicated than was once believed. Like the cells of our body itself, they are systems of tiny organs, and contain the same chemical compounds that make up our genes, the small cells which transmit hereditary traits from parents to children.

Many people tend to think of bacteria as unpleasant disease-producers. This is not so. Scientists have shown that they can be "domesticated" to the service of man by producing reactions that yield beer, tasty cheese and valuable medicine.

The modern study of them has shown that they suffer from virus diseases just as we do. So a close look at their defences may help scientists in their fight against the viruses which attack us.

Just how widespread bacteria are was

The father of microscopy was Anton Leeuwenhoek (below) who, in 1683, became the first man to see bacteria through a microscope of his own invention. On the left is a 17th century microscope believed to have been used by Robert Hooke, an English scientist.

shown in an experiment in which a culture plate with an area of seven and a half square inches was left on a clean staircase landing.

At the end of one hour, ninety-five disease-carrying and other types of bacteria were found to have settled on it.

The story of man's first observation of bacteria through microscopes is an amazing story, not as you might expect of a great scientist, nor of a great chemist, but of a completely unknown Dutch cloth merchant with a most unusual hobby.

His name was Anton van Leeuwenhoek, and he is sometimes called the father of microscopy. He lived three hundred years ago.

Van Leeuwenhoek's hobby was the study of bacteria. He would watch them born, divide, multiply and die. And he did this with a microscope he developed himself after he had found the existing forms of magnification too imperfect for his purposes.

Scientists before him had used a single convex lens, probably based upon their observation of how a drop of rain magnified a leaf it rested upon. At the end of the 16th century, Dutch spectacle makers found that two lenses placed some inches apart gave an even more powerful magnification of minute insects. So the first compound microscope was built.

Leeuwenhoek was determined to produce something better. After many disappointments, he found a way of manufacturing a tiny bead of glass and setting it in a metal plate.

He then mounted the specimens he wanted to examine on an adjustable pointer. This was a return to the simple convex lens. It worked so well that van Leeuwenhoek was able to magnify his specimens up to 250 times, and in 1683 he became the first man to see bacteria.

With the gradual improvement of the lenses and the methods of construction in the years that followed, the microscope became the trade mark of scientists and, in particular, biologists.

Today, it is one of the few pieces of equipment that is found in every type of biological laboratory and it has revolutionised the science of unlocking the inner secrets of life.

The average human eye is just able to see two separate objects that are 0·07 millimetres apart. If they are closer than that, they appear as one object and any details on them that are smaller than 0·07 millimetres are lost. In order to see any objects smaller than this, a microscope must be used.

Some of van Leeuwenhoek's lenses had a magnifying power of up to 250 times, but it was impossible to use them to see objects 1/250th of 0·07 millimetres because, like all simple lenses, they suffered from optical

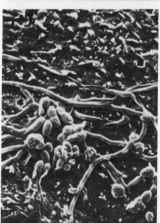

A new world is revealed through the electron microscope. Above is a sample of "fur" scraped from the inside of a kettle.

Fungus and spores can be seen on the surface of an apple (left) and are about to penetrate the fruit.

Below is a hyperdermic needle magnified considerably. It looks far more formidable like this than when viewed life-size.

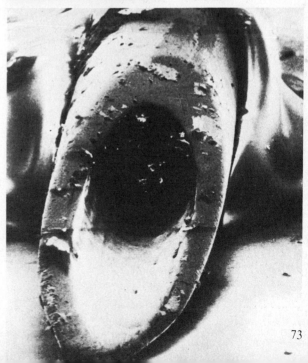

Microscopes underwent a real revolution in 1940 with the commercial development of the first electron microscope that brought about a tremendous increase in magnification.

defects. These could make squares look barrel-shaped or like pin-cushions and cause variations in colour and in focusing powers.

Even today, with precision polishing and grinding machines for making lenses, these defects still appear and have to be rectified inside a microscope by using many lenses, each designed to cancel out a certain optical fault and thereby produce an accurate image.

It was in 1940 that a real revolution occurred in microscopes which made possible the study of cells and minute organisms. It was then that the first *electron* microscopes were commercially developed.

Up to that date, the maximum magnification possible with a compound light microscope was 1500x. Above this power, whatever lenses are used, the microscope is useless because light waves themselves are about one-fifty-thousandth of an inch long, which prevents objects smaller than that from being seen.

The electron microscope overcomes this difficulty by using a beam of electrons, the tiny particles from which electricity is made, instead of a beam of light. And instead of lenses, it uses powerful electro-magnets for focusing the beam.

Although invisible, the beam affects a fluorescent screen and produces an image in much the same way as pictures are built up on the inside of a coated television screen. The beam can also be directed on to photographic film to produce a visible image.

The electron microscope can produce pictures with a direct magnification of 20,000x. The film can then be enlarged to give a further magnification of 100,000x.

The operator views the fluorescent screen inside the electron microscope through a pair of binoculars, looking through a lead-glass window which shields him from the X-rays that the machine emits.

The electron beam itself is produced by heating to white heat a tungsten filament at the top of the microscope. The specimen is mounted on a tiny perforated copper grid covered by a layer of plastic a few molecules thick, and the beam passes through it to create the image on the fluorescent screen.

Particles that are only four millionths of an inch in size can be detected by the most

An electron microscope (above and below) can produce pictures with a magnification of 20,000 times and the film can then be enlarged to give a further magnification of 100,000 times.

Right: a cutaway sketch of an electron microscope. A beam of electrons is focused by magnets on to the specimen, through which it passes on to a fluorescent screen, like that in a TV set.

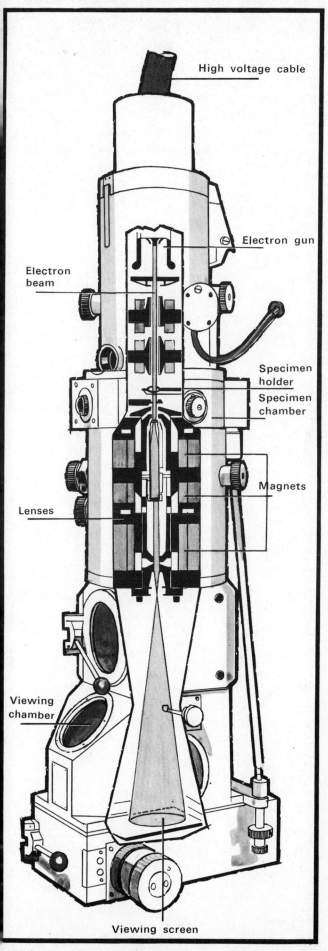

High voltage cable

Electron gun

Electron beam

Specimen holder

Specimen chamber

Magnets

Lenses

Viewing chamber

Viewing screen

powerful electron microscopes, and minute foreign bodies in human or other animal tissue, which formerly defied detection, can now be seen.

The image produced by the conventional electron microscope is two dimensional, flat, like a picture without any depth or perspective. But an electron microscope which is three-dimensional has been developed in Britain.

Called the "stereoscan", it sacrifices some of the clarity of the ordinary microscopes in order to get a picture which has depth. For some types of research, the sacrifice is worthwhile because surfaces can be seen in much greater detail.

It opens up a world that adds new knowledge and dimensions to scientific research, and it has been made possible through the discovery of the electron by Sir J. J. Thomson in 1897.

He discovered that when two metal plates were sealed into a glass tube, from which all air had been exhausted, a stream of rays flowed from the negative plate to the positive plate.

The rays consisted of negatively charged particles, which were named electrons. Their action is used with striking effect in a special kind of electron microscope. This is called the field emission microscope. It is capable of magnification so great that it is possible to see the individual atoms forming the molecules of a substance.

A molecule is the smallest particle that can exist without changing its nature. For instance, a salt particle has one atom of sodium and one atom of chlorine. To make it any smaller, you would have to separate these two atoms.

The field emission microscope is worked by the application of a high voltage to a metal tip inside a vacuum tube. When the electrons stream from the tip, they create a magnified pattern of it on a screen.

The discovery of the microscope, and the amazing developments that have followed it, have opened up a new world of understanding to us. At a magnification of 50,000 times, a hair from your head would look as big as a factory chimney. A tennis ball would be two miles in diameter!

But its real value lies in our being able to study the structure of matter, to increase our knowledge of organic and inorganic substances, and to improve our ability to conquer disease.

Probably the microscope's greatest triumphs were made in the hands of Louis Pasteur and his work which led to the beginning of modern medical hygiene.

But there have been important discoveries made with it since—and undoubtedly there will be more to follow.

Visitors from space

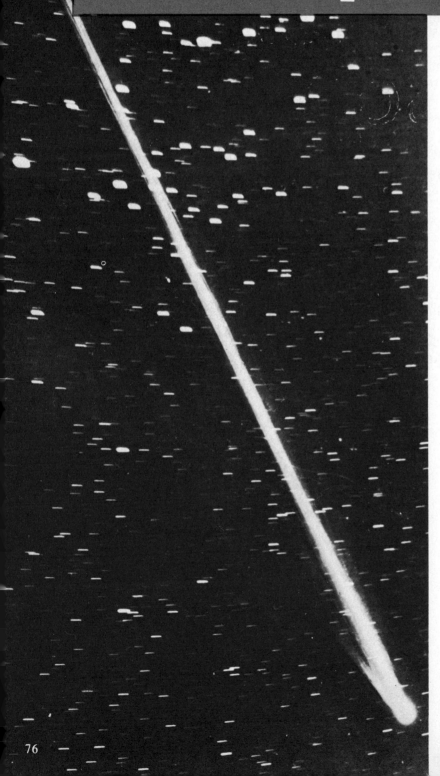

Reports of visitors from space have aroused excited speculation in the newspapers in recent years. While these may have been based more upon fancy than fact, it is true that one type of visitor, at least, has been regularly landing upon our planet.

OVER the past few decades there have been many reports of so-called 'flying saucers' and other mysterious space vehicles which are said to have landed on our planet. Some of these extra-terrestial machines have even been said to contain little 'men' who were visiting Earth, for reasons which no one has been able to explain.

Whatever the truth of these sightings, one thing we can be sure about is that the only 'visitors from space' which have left any real evidence of their arrival are *meteorites*.

Apart from *meteorites*,

A comet streaks through space, leaving behind it a visible tail of incandescence.

there are also *meteors,* and *meteoroids,* so it is as well to understand what these other words mean.

When some object from outer space enters the earth's atmosphere at high speed, the friction resulting from its movement through the gases causes it to heat up rapidly until it glows first red, and ultimately white hot. It also leaves behind it a visible trail of incandesence that can clearly be seen at night.

These objects have often been called 'shooting stars', but they are really meteors, which is the name given to the trial of luminosity they create. The object itself is known as a meteoroid, and if it finally succeeds in reaching the surface of the

This enormous crater was formed 20,000 years ago when a meteor crashed to earth in Arizona. Scientists believe it to be similar to craters on the Moon.

earth without being burned completely away, it is called a meteorite.

The command modules of American Apollo space ships glow like meteors soon after re-entry into the earth's atmosphere, but unlike meteorites, they are fitted with special parachutes to slow them down so that they can 'soft-land' in the sea.

Meteorites are usually travelling at many thousands of miles an hour when they enter the atmosphere, and

apart from some loss of speed due to the friction, they are still moving at very high speeds when they strike the ground.

So fast are they travelling, and so hot are some of them when they arrive that they explode and vaporize on impact with the earth.

The few witnesses who have been close enough to hear a meteorite approaching the earth have described the sound it makes as like a series of loud thunder claps, followed by a roaring noise such as you might hear from an express train.

Anybody struck by a meteorite may well be seriously injured or even killed, but the chances of this happening are extremely remote, and far less likely than being struck by lightning.

It is impossible to say exactly now many meteorites actually strike the earth's surface. As approximately four fifth's of our planet is covered by water, many must fall unseen into the oceans, but scientists have calculated that about 150 of these visitors from space fall each year on to the land-covered areas.

✻ ✻ ✻ ✻

Many meteorites must fall on uninhabited areas, and their arrival goes unnoticed, but it would seem from an examination of recorded findings that they do not fall in particular areas of the world, and their distribution is quite random.

Meteorites vary greatly in size, from those weighing a few ounces to giants of

It is reasonable to assume that meteorites are the result of the break-up of a planet which once formed part of the solar system.

100 tons. The larger ones form craters; the most spectacular of these was found in 1891 in Arizona, U.S.A. It is about three-quarters of a mile in diameter, nearly 600 feet deep, and was the result of a meteorite which fell in pre-historic times.

The massive meteorite that caused the huge crater was never found and it is assumed that it must have disintegrated on impact. Small meteorites were discovered scattered around outside the crater up to a distance of six miles.

Another large meteorite, weighing one ton, was found in a place called Hoba in

south west Africa many years ago. The Hoba meteorite is composed of a nickel-iron alloy. These two metals form the main constituents of most meteorites, although others that are found are of a stony nature.

✻ ✻ ✻ ✻

Scientists believe that the earth consists of a solid core of nickel-iron surrounded by the same alloy in a molten state. Between this layer and the outer crust is a mantle of silicate rocks, so it is reasonable to assume that meteorites are the result of the break-up of a planet which once formed part of the solar system, as they are of the same material.

The millions of particles which once were a whole planet are still orbiting the Sun, and from time to time the Earth crosses their path and a shower of them enter the atmosphere.

Meteorite showers can sometimes be spectacular events, especially when seen at night. These showers or swarms appear to fall from a single point in the heavens which astronomers call the 'radiant', and the showers are named after the constellation in which the radiant appears to lie.

This meteorite, weighing 21·6 pounds, was recovered near Lost City, Oklahoma, U.S.A. on 9th January, 1970, following its entry into the Earth's atmosphere on 3rd January.

The world's fifth largest iron meteorite (right) was discovered in Greenland in 1963 by a Danish scientist who estimated its weight as 18 tons.

The big picture on this page is of a model of the Moon, reproducing its appearance from a space ship about ten miles above the surface. All the craters on the Moon are believed to have been made by meteorites.

OUR WONDERFUL WORLD OF SCIENCE QUIZ

Now that you have read Our Wonderful World of Science, you will want to test your knowledge with the questions below. See how many you can answer.

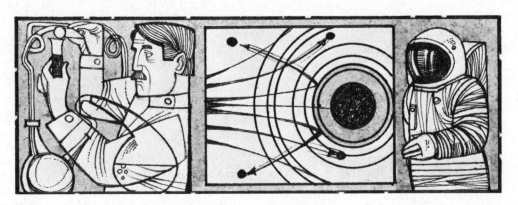

1. Sponge divers were the first to explore the sea's depths. What did they collect in addition to sponges?

2. What parts of the human body are most affected by the pressure of the water at great depths?

3. An unwanted gas gets into one's bloodstream at great sea depths. Can you name this gas?

4. In theory, glass is stronger than steel, but is it a liquid or a solid?

5. Aircraft canopies are made of laminated glass. What kind of glass is this?

6. Researchers in Arizona have built a heat telescope. What does it do?

7. A Space launching vehicle that may be re-used many times is being developed in the U.S.A. Can you name it?

8. What is the name of a vehicle that will be able to fly in the Earth's atmosphere or travel in Space?

9. Beneath the ground are stores of fuel known as fossil sources. Can you name two fuels we get from these?

10. The energy we get from food is measured in calories. What are calories?

11. What are the two elements of which coal, oil and natural gas are mostly made?

12. Can you give the collective name for uranium, thorium and plutonium?

13. Energy is measured in units. What is the name of these units?

14. What are the only "visitors" from Outer Space to have left evidence of their arrival?

15. How many of these are calculated to fall on land-covered areas each year?

16. What is the substance of which the Earth's core is made?

17. Anton van Leeuwenhoek was a Dutch cloth merchant. But for what work is he more famous?

18. What piece of optical equipment is to be found in every type of biological laboratory?

19. What invention in 1940 made possible the study of cells and minute organisms?

20. When negatively charged particles flow from one plate to another in a vacuum, what are they called? Who discovered this effect in 1897?

THE ANSWERS ARE AT THE BACK OF THE BOOK.

Bandits, Indians and hungry wolves were among the hazards which beset stage coach travellers.

WHEELS ACROSS THE WEST

Stagecoach travel was no joyride in the days of the American West when ruthless bandits and marauding Indians turned each journey into a dangerous adventure.

"It's a hold-up!" Cracking his whip furiously, the stagecoach driver warns his colleague as he spots a fast-moving group of riders.

The horses increase their speed; their manes flare out like angry flames as panic spurs them on to even greater effort. A cloud of swirling dust marks the trail of the coach across the prairie as the thundering wheels race for their life.

But help is at hand!

Silhouetted against the skyline is a solitary figure astride his faithful wonder horse. Our hero! Dashing to

Passengers, beginning their journey in a township (left) were rarely prepared for the startling sights they could see on the trail (above).

the rescue he outguns the gang of desperadoes pursuing the coach, saves the passengers and, eventually, rides off into the sunset with the heroine at his side.

* * * *

It is a scene familiar to all filmgoers. But the Hollywood western tends to over-romanticise the pioneering days of early America, for it was nowhere near as glamorous as the film makers would have you believe. Stagecoach travel, for example, was extremely rough and rugged. During the summer months temperatures in the dust-laden interior of the coach often rose to a sticky 110°F and over. In winter the inadequate leather curtains fought a losing battle against the snow which flew through the open windows onto the freezing occupants. With temperatures that frequently

fell below zero passengers were faced with the continual problem of keeping themselves warm. Liberal doses of whisky eased the situation for the men but women, who were forbidden to drink in public, had to face the rigours of winter travel unaided.

With "a fat man on one side, a poor widow on the other, a baby in your lap and a hatbox over your

head" all the way from the Pacific to the Atlantic states stagecoach travel was no joyride. Overflow luggage and mail was packed inside the coach along with the unfortunate passengers. Overcrowding was a problem outside as well as inside; on the roof of the coach other passengers clung precariously during the long, bumpy and arduous journey.

And the refreshment stops were

When rivers had to be forded, the passengers got out and helped the coach to trundle through the water.

A wheel broken on the rugged trail was just one of the many mishaps that could delay a journey.

* * * *
Travellers were offered what pretended to be tea. But Mark Twain said there was too much dishrag, sand and old bacon rind in it to deceive the intelligent passenger.
* * * *

no picnics either. At the remote and primitive stations where the horses were changed the passengers were offered unappetising meals of "tough beef, beans, greasy potatoes, venison and an occasional apple pie with coffee strong enough to float a mule shoe." If you preferred to drink tea you could have what Mark Twain described as slugmullion which "pretended to be tea, but there was too much dishrag and sand, and old bacon rind in it to deceive the intelligent passenger."

Sleep, almost an impossibility, had to be snatched whilst the stage was on the move. For three long weeks there was no chance of a bath and little opportunity to change one's clothing. It is little wonder that by the time they had reached their destination the passengers felt like limp, and exceedingly dirty, rags. As one passenger remarked: "I know what hell is like, I've just had twenty-four days of it."

Rough travelling conditions were not the only problems passengers had to contend with—there were also bandits and Indians. Before the journey travellers were warned, "You will be travelling through Indian country and the safety of your person

cannot be vouchsafed by anyone but God." They were advised to arm themselves with a Sharp's rifle, a hundred rounds of ammunition, a Colt's Navy revolver and two pounds of shot.

* * * *

Other necessities for the journey were "a pair of thick boots and woollen pants; a half dozen pairs of thick woollen socks; six undershirts; a wide-awake hat; a cheap sack coat; a soldier's overcoat; one pair of blankets in summer and two in winter; a piece of India rubber cloth; a pair of gauntlets; a small bag of needles; pins, sponge, hairbrush, comb, soap, etc. in an oil silk bag; two pairs of thick drawers and three or four towels."

Although by the early 1850s there were many stagecoach routes and stage companies, there was no overland connection between the Pacific states and the Atlantic states. Mail

sent from one side of America to the other had to go by boat around Cape Horn. The settlers in California were on their own, virtually cut off from the rest of the country.

Public protestation at this lack of efficient transport spurred Congress to authorise the Postmaster General to invite tenders for the provision of a cross-country mail and passenger service. John Butterfield, president of the newly formed Overland Mail Company, was awarded the contract.

On 16 September, 1858, the Overland Company's first west and eastbound transcontinental stages began their inaugural treks. Stretching for 2,800 miles the route selected by the Postmaster, later to become famous as the 'Ox Bow Route', went far south and included many desert stretches where the going was extra tough with water in such short supply. But, even so, both of the first two coaches arrived on time. On 11 October the streets of San Francisco wore a carnival atmosphere

to welcome the westbound stage—
an atmosphere matched only by that
in Tipton on the other side of the
continent when the eastbound coach
also arrived on schedule.

✳ ✳ ✳ ✳

Bankers and part owners of the
Overland were the Wells Fargo
Company formed by Henry Wells
of Vermont and William Fargo of
New York on 18 March, 1852. Their
main business was banking; services
offered by their first office at 114
Montgomery Street in the hustling,
bustling city of San Francisco,
included the buying and selling of
gold, silver and bullion, banking and
exchange.

By 1 November 1866, Wells Fargo
had gained complete control of the
Overland Mail Company and its
routes from the Missouri to the
Pacific in addition to many thousands
of miles of stagecoach lines in other
parts of the country. Today it is the
name of Wells Fargo that is most
closely associated with the era of the
American stagecoach.

But the years were numbered for
the stage. The day of the stagecoach
driver, called 'Jehu' after the Biblical
character, was drawing to a close.
His place was being taken by the
train driver. Across the prairie could
be heard the shrill sound of train
whistles—the death knell of the
stagecoach. The 'iron road' was
sweeping over the country to provide
faster, more efficient and more
comfortable travel than the stagecoach could ever hope to offer.

✳ ✳ ✳ ✳

The final blow was delivered on
10 May, 1869 when, at Promontory
Point, Utah, two sections of track
were joined to complete an unbroken
line of iron from east to west.

Leland Stanford, president of the
Central Pacific Railway, was the man
destined to kill the stagecoach on
that cold May afternoon. The final
spike, linking the two sections of
railroad, had attached to it a
telegraph wire. To the hammer was
affixed a second wire so that the
blows could be heard throughout the
nation. Stanford raised the hammer
above his head. The watching crowd
of Irish and Chinese railway workers,
saloon girls and sightseers, held their
breath. It was a great moment in the
history of America. Stanford brought
the hammer down towards the stake
—and missed!

But, although the historic hammer
missed, the era of the stagecoach had
reached its sad end. Today it lives on
in the cinema. Although, over-
glamorised, the stagecoach on film
will provide a long lasting reminder
of a form of travel the like of which
may never be seen again.

**Horses were
sometimes changed in
desolate places
(above). Even where
there was a
refreshment cabin,
the food was poor and
unappetising (right).
After this, the
traveller's destination,
below, was always a
welcome sight.**

The Greeks loved to listen to Homer, the great story-teller. One of the tales he told was of how, four hundred years earlier, the Greek warriors had set out to conquer the city of Troy. However, they were unable to get past the city walls until they discovered a way of doing so by building an enormous wooden horse and tricking the Trojans with this.

THE TROJAN HORSE~ FACT OR FICTION?

Heinrich Schliemann plunged his spade into the soil. It struck something hard beneath the earth, and the vibrations it made quivered through Schliemann's body. Eagerly, he shovelled away the soil and brought into view stone that had not seen the light of day for centuries. It was a stupendous historical find. Schliemann had found the ancient city of Troy.

The year was 1870. At intervals during the following twenty years Schliemann, and teams of up to 150 workmen, scraped away the soil from the foundations of the city made famous by the epic poems of Homer, the Greek poet, and Virgil, his

After dark, while Troy slept, the Greek warriors climbed out of the wooden horse, overpowered the city's sentries and let in the Greek army which was waiting outside. And Troy, after resisting a long siege, was finally defeated.

Roman counterpart. These tell of the wars between the Greeks and the Trojans, and a ten-year siege of Troy that was ended by a remarkable ruse.

Schliemann made his discovery upon a hill called Hissarlik. This stands above the Dardanelles, a long, narrow strait connecting the Aegean Sea with the Sea of Marmara in Asia Minor. He found that nine cities or settlements, each built successively upon the ruins of its predecessor, were erected here.

The second city is believed to be the one pictured in the poems. It was built by labourers, carpenters and masons of blocks of squared stone, and bricks made crudely with mud and straw. Its houses had wooden timbers and beams and they were roofed with clay and thatch. There were temples and palaces beside the humbler homes, all surrounded by a strong wall to keep out invaders.

It was outside these walls that the Greeks encamped for ten years, maintaining a siege that neither side could break.

Eventually, the Greeks hit upon a brilliant idea for getting into the city. One of their number, named Epeus, proposed building a wooden horse, big enough to accommodate several fighters within its hollow inside.

According to tradition, it was made from the wood of a species of cherry tree called cornel that grew on Mount Ida. Virgil, however, says that it was made of planks of pine and was of "monstrous height".

When it was finished, several fighters climbed into its hollow interior.

Leaving behind them the enormous horse, the rest of the Greek fleet sailed away. Once the coast was clear, the Trojans came out of their city and found the horse with, near it, a Greek named Sinon.

He was an undercover agent for the Greeks, and his story was that he had been chosen as a human sacrifice to ensure good weather for the return home of the Greek fleet. Fortunately, he had escaped from the altar to

Left: a picture of Mycenaean soldiers painted three thousand years ago. King Agamemnon, who was the leader of the Greeks in the Trojan war, was supposed to have been murdered at Mycenae by his wife, but his grave has not been discovered. Right: an ivory head of a Greek warrior. Several men, looking as tough as this, are said to have hidden inside the wooden horse.

which he had been tied, and now threw himself upon the Trojans' mercy.

The Trojans gave the horse a mixed reception. Some wanted to smash it or throw it into the sea. Others wanted to drag it into their city. One of them thrust his spear into the horse's side, and another said that it was an engine of war designed to bring about their defeat.

Sinon calmed their fears by saying that the horse had been left as a peace offering to the goddess Pallas Athena, the protectress of Greek cities.

It was made too big to be taken through the city gates, said Sinon, because a prophet named Calchas had warned the Greeks that if the horse were taken into Troy it would bring about the defeat of the Greeks by the Trojans at their next encounter. If it was damaged, however, the Trojans would be the ones to suffer a disaster.

It was the first prophecy that clinched the matter for the Trojans. If the horse was going to bring them victory in war if it went into their city, into their city it would go.

By breaking a lintel over one of the city gates, they managed to enlarge the opening sufficiently to drag the horse inside, regardless of the clanging of armour that came from its interior as they did so.

After dark, when the Trojans were asleep, Sinon crept out of the city to watch for the return of the Greek fleet. When a light was lit to show him that they were ready for battle, Sinon crept up to the wooden horse, unbarred a secret door, and let out the soldiers from within.

They overpowered the sentries and opened all the city gates. The returned Greek soldiers rushed into Troy, killed all the men, captured the women as slaves and ransacked and pillaged until the city was in ruins.

This is the story as told by Virgil and Homer. All that we know about the wooden horse has come down to us in their poems. However, archaeologists have discovered that Troy and other famous cities such as Mycenae, from where King Agamemnon ruled a vast kingdom, really did exist.

Perhaps the wars also took place as Homer and Virgil described them. And perhaps the wooden horse, too, was fact and not fiction? Such ruses have been used in wars since, and could have been used then.

However, we may never know the truth of this, for wood perishes. And if the wooden horse existed, the last fragment of it rotted away long ago.

The only slight evidence as to its existence is at Trebisacce, a town in the heel of the Italian boot, where there are said to be the tools that were used in the construction of the wooden horse. Historians who dispute this quote the Roman scholar Justinus as saying that they are in the temple of Minerva, a Roman goddess of war, at Metaponto in Italy, which was the Greek city of Metapontum.

Homer lived in the 8th century B.C. Virgil lived from 70 to 19 B.C. The events they describe are set in a period many hundreds of years earlier. While their poems are a valuable contribution to literature, their value as historical records is difficult to prove.

However, if some of the facts they contain are correct, perhaps others, such as those relating to the wooden horse, can be accepted also.

When Schliemann found Troy, he established some of the facts as historically correct. He then set out to prove others. King Agamemnon was the leader of the Greeks in the Trojan war. He was murdered at Mycenae by his wife, whom he had discarded in favour of a Trojan princess. So says the legend. Schliemann wanted to find King Agamemnon's grave. If he was successful, the legends would have further authenticity.

He began digging for the Homeric king within a circle of upright stones just within the walls of Mycenae. The ruins of this are well known. They stand on top of a pale outcrop of rock in the plain of Argos, guarding the pass between two great, blue-shadowed mountains.

Schliemann found six shaft-graves, each with several skeletons and accompanied by golden crowns, gold-hilted daggers, jewellery and seals. Sheets of gold had been laid over the faces of the male skeletons.

Several of the faces superimposed on the gold sheets were just eyes and nose and mouth. But one face in particular had been carefully moulded to reveal a moustache and a beard. When Schliemann lifted this mask, he saw that the face underneath it was strangely preserved with all its flesh. Soon after being exposed to the air, however, it crumbled away.

At the sight of it, Schliemann started back. "I have looked upon the face of Agamemnon," he declared in a trembling voice.

Unfortunately, he was wrong. The shaft graves he had discovered were those of the Mycenean kings who had lived very much later, between 1700 and 1500 B.C.

Perhaps Schliemann was too hasty and not very scholarly in his methods. But he proved that some of the places mentioned by Virgil and Homer really did exist. Perhaps those exciting, clamorous wars of the epic poems really were fought?

Punch and Judy is a familiar sight in Britain, but where did it come from?

Hello, Mister Punch!

It is a warm summer's day. A group of happy, laughing children are sitting on the beach looking in eager anticipation at a red and white striped, canvas-covered booth. The show is about to begin.

There is a fanfare of trumpets, the children stop chatting, the curtains open, and a funny figure with a big nose makes his welcome appearance in the miniature theatre. The children cheer and clap their familiar friend, resplendent in his red and yellow finery. "Hello, children" he cries in a squeaky, nasal voice. "Hello, Mr. Punch" the children reply in unison—and the show is on.

A large part of the Punch and Judy performance consists of a series of what seem rather cruel scenes: Punch beats his wife; she in turn bashes him. A baby is beaten with a stick and batted out of the tiny theatre like a cricket ball. A policeman appears on the scene and is soundly clubbed by Mr. Punch; a similar fate awaits an unfortunate crocodile. And yet, in spite of all this violence, the Punch and Judy show remains one of the most popular forms of entertainment.

Punch and Judy is a familiar sight in Britain, but where did it come from? How did Punch get his name? Is he really English? The clue to the answers to these, and similar, questions can be found on a plaque outside St. Paul's Church in London's Covent Garden which states: "Near this spot Punch's Puppet Show was first performed in England—1662."

Samuel Pepys mentions this puppet show in his famous diary when, on 9th May, 1662, he went to Covent Garden, "to see an Italian puppet play that is within the rails there which is very pretty, the best that I ever saw."

Pietro Gimonde from Bologna in Italy was the owner of

When Pietro Gimonde brought his puppet show to London he introduced his audience to a hook-nosed character who was to become familiar as Mr. Punch.

this show that was destined to have such a profound effect on the English puppet scene. His appearance in London is generally acknowledged as the introduction to British audiences of the character who was to become Punch. The hero of the performance was a hook-nosed clown called Pollicinella, famous throughout Europe for his amusing antics and ready wit.

But Pollicinella, too, has quite a history. It stretches back over two thousand years—through the Italian puppet shows based on the Commedia dell'Arte in the early 1600s, and the itinerant puppet performers that roamed Europe for over a thousand years—to the Roman and Greek puppet shows that were popular in ancient times.

England, also, had an active puppet tradition stemming from the Greek and Roman puppet theatres. This proud tradition, merged with English folklore and the mystery plays of the early English church, helped to produce a unique and active puppet theatre.

When the European puppeteers started visiting England, the two traditions combined to create the early ancestors of Punch. These new and exciting puppet personalities went under various names—Pollicinella, Pulcina, Polichinelle, Punchinello, and Punctionella. The English, unable to cope with these continental tongue-twisters, shortened the whole lot into one, easily remembered name—Punch.

Punch's lively, arrogant character caught the public's fancy, and before long he was featured in almost every puppet show. He became so popular that in the early 1700s there was established in London a theatre devoted solely to Punch and called, appropriately, 'Punch's Theatre'.

The owner of Punch's Theatre was Martin Powell, a successful showman from the fairs that were a regular feature of the English way of life. Powell also wrote the plays performed by his miniature actors but his main claim to fame in the story of our hero is that he appears to have been the first to give Punch a wife. Her original name was Joan, but through the years this has gradually changed to Judy.

Towards the end of the 18th century puppet popularity began to wane. Puppet performers, faced with falling attendances, left the fairs in which they had been appearing and took to the road to perform when and where someone would stop to watch. The marionettes, puppets worked by strings, that they had been using had to be abandoned, and glove puppets took their place.

Mr. Punch, too, had to change with the times, and so became a glove puppet along with his fellows. The nature of the puppeteer's new working environment, travelling from town to town, brought about this change. Glove puppets were cheaper to support, they only needed one operator whereas marionette shows used several, and no elaborate theatre, or 'set-up', was required.

During the 18th century the seaside holiday became popular and so the puppet men, always in search of a paying audience, carried their shows to the coast. Punch and Judy shows have found appreciative audiences on many English beaches ever since.

In May, 1962, on the three hundredth anniversary of Punch's first appearance in the British Isles, showmen from all over Great Britain gathered in London.

After attending a service at St. Paul's Church, Covent Garden, they went outside where they saw, against the wall of the church, an enormous Punch and Judy booth. As the curious showmen approached the booth Mr. Punch made an unexpected appearance, his stick at the ready to deal with any adversary. Following a short repartee with a clown, another popular figure from the puppet theatre, he tapped three times with his stick. An explosion of gabbling, babbling Punch figures burst suddenly into view. Forty of them filled the stage with a myriad of colours and caco-

Unlike the marionette show which used several operators the Punch and Judy show could be operated by one man.

phonous chattering, to be joined a moment later by forty Judys singing and dancing merrily.

The festivities continued with the production of a birthday cake bearing fireworks for candles, from which crocodiles, snakes, and dragons sprang forth. A golden cord was pulled by the puppets. Pulling together like a tiny tug o' war team they revealed the plaque on the wall of the church commemorating three hundred years of the most famous of puppet characters—Punch.

They ate a 20-year-old-stew.

Nicholas Appert found a way of preserving food in jars by heating it after the jar had been stoppered. His discovery paved the way for an industry that was to be a boon to mankind.

Dr. Alfred S. Taylor peered at the chemistry students ranged on rows of seats before him in the lecture room of Guy's Hospital in London. ''This is the moment of revelation,'' he said with a slight smile, and picked up a hammer and chisel.

He placed the chisel upon the object on the table before him and struck it smartly with the hammer. Within a few seconds, the operation had been successfully

''This is the moment of revelation,'' said Dr. Taylor with a slight smile, as he opened the 20-years-old tin of stew.

91

performed. Dr. Taylor had opened a tin of stewed meat.

He sniffed the contents, said that they smelled fresh, and then gave his hearers a lecture about the value of the then little-known canning process, promising to give them a chemical analysis of the contents after he had had a chance to test them later.

Unfortunately, he had on his staff some hungry assistants, who ate the meat before it could be analysed. As they suffered no ill-effects from their stolen meal, Dr. Taylor was able to conclude that the contents of the can had been edible.

This was an inglorious end to an historic can of meat that had been part of the stores of H.M.S. "Blonde" which went on a voyage of discovery to the Sandwich Isles in 1826. It was superfluous to the ship's needs and finally came into the hands of Dr. Taylor. By the time he was prepared to examine it, the tin was twenty years old. His analysis of its

contents would have been a testimony to the excellence of British canned goods, had it been possible for him to make one.

Forty years earlier, Nicholas Appert had discovered a way of preserving food in jars by heating it after the jar had been stoppered. The use of cans instead of jars came soon afterwards.

At first, the cans were made by hand, fifty a day being a good average for one man. And the lids were soldered on also by hand after the tins had been filled. Since can openers had not been invented, it was necessary to open the cans with a hammer and chisel, like those used by Dr. Taylor.

Explorers and sailors were especially grateful to the youthful canning industry, for it enabled them to have a greater variety of food than their usual salt beef and dry biscuit. Cans of food went voyaging around the world with scores of intrepid explorers. Admiral Cochrane

Nicholas Appert, the man who discovered the art of preserving food in jars.

enjoyed canned food in St. Helena in 1814; the Duke of Wellington added canned meat to his rations in 1813, and Sir Edward Parry enjoyed some while he was leading an expedition in search of the North-West Passage in 1819.

In fact, the tracks of British military men and explorers, whether in the deserts or the polar wastes, are strewn with tin cans, now hidden under layers of sand or ice.

This has been made possible by Appert's discovery that if he heated food in some sort of sealed jar it would keep for a long time. But it was not until Pasteur discovered the facts about bacteria that we understood why food remained fresh after this treatment.

It does so, we have discovered, because nearly all the bacteria in the can are killed by heat which is applied to them. The conditions in the tin are unfavourable to the growth of those left alive, and they cannot do any harm.

Sir Edward Parry (pictured left) included canned food in his rations while searching for the North-West passage, 1819.

Jars of food bottled by Appert were tried out by the French Navy in about 1806, and in 1810 he published a book on the art of preserving food. This was read in Britain with great interest by John Hall, who was the founder of an iron works. He foresaw a fine future for his firm if metal containers could be used instead of glass. Hall's associate, Bryan Donkin, is thought to have been the one who found a successful way of preserving food in tins, and is regarded as the father of the modern canning industry.

After a few years of experiments and failures, Donkin and Hall's factory was sending tins of food to the Army and Navy for trials, and some of it was taken on overseas expeditions. Cans of meat and soup went with John Ross, who made many explorations to the Arctic. On an expedition to Baffin's Bay, Greenland, in 1814, Ross noted in his diary that the canned food was given to the men after the fresh vegetables had been eaten.

By 1818, canned foods had become a vital part of the stores of ships of the British Navy, by whom they were chiefly used to prevent scurvy. For a long time, the use of canned food was confined to the Army, the Navy, and explorers who were likely to be out of reach of fresh food.

A big exhibition held in London in 1851 helped to get them better known. But what gave them a big boost was the First World War of 1914-1918 when millions of tins of meat and vegetable stew were produced for feeding the troops.

Soldiers, having canned food in the front line, were willing to eat it at home. However, there was a great deal of poverty in the post-war years. Despite this, there was a gradual growth in the use of canned food in the home until, today, many millions of cans are sold every year in Britain alone.

Other methods of preservation, such as freezing and drying, have failed to replace canning as a means of providing a quick meal. Modern methods of production ensure that the contents are always pure and nutritious.

Unfortunately, in the early days, this was not always the case. One firm obtained a contract in 1845 to supply canned food for an expedition by Rear Admiral Sir John Franklin in his ships, "Erebus" and "Terror" which were to explore the North-West Passage. During this adventure, Franklin disappeared.

Later expeditions were sent out to find traces of him, and records were found to show that he had died in 1847. One of the searchers, Captain Ommanney, discovered on Beechey Island stacks of provisions which Franklin had abandoned. Among them were canisters which contained rotten meat.

Captain Ommanney said that they had been filled with "putrid abomination . . . thus fatally diminishing the three

Pasteur discovered that heating a can of food killed nearly all harmful bacteria.

years' provisions which were supposed to be on board".

Franklin's own records, found in a cairn on the ice, showed that he had discovered the North-West Passage, a route from the Atlantic to the Pacific through the Arctic Seas.

He did not live to claim the credit for this. That honour was to go to Roald Amundsen who made the complete voyage between 1903 and 1905. Perhaps Franklin would have lived to earn the recognition for his achievement had the canning industry been as efficient then as it is now.

When the guilty canning firm applied for another Admiralty contract, one curt word was written upon their application : "declined".

It pronounced the sentence of death upon a bad supplier and left the way clear for the efficient ones that were to follow.

Not all canned foods were successful as Rear Admiral Sir John Franklin found when he had to dump provisions during his fatal exploration of the North-West passage.

TERROR

It must have been the strangest procession of all time, unusual even for an 18th century London where horror often went hand-in-hand with merriment.

Along the streets packed with milling crowds there came a line of marching constables. Then came a dignified sheriff in his chariot pulled by six horses which had black mourning ribbons tied to their harness.

Behind these came the central figure in the parade, a nobleman named Lord Ferrers who was chatting to a clergyman who sat beside him, as if he had not a care in the world.

Then came an empty coach, its six horses happy at the lightness of their load. This was owned by another sheriff who, when he was not on duty, was a French bookseller named M. Vaillant, who had a shop in the Strand.

Instead of being in his own coach, however, M. Vaillant was travelling with Lord Ferrers—as a guard.

A macabre touch was added by the procession's final vehicle—a hearse containing an empty coffin. Lord Ferrers was going to make the return journey in the coffin.

You would not have suspected this from the gaiety of his manner, because he waved and smiled at the crowds, who cheered in reply. And when M. Vaillant told him to behave as soberly as the rest of the people in the procession, Lord Ferrers replied, "The populace are seeing a peer of the realm going to his execution, a sight they are never, perhaps, likely to enjoy a second

AT TYBURN

time." M. Vaillant did not care for the use of the word "enjoy".

It was true that the mob lining the route got a great deal of pleasure out of seeing people going to their doom. In this case, Laurence Shirley Ferrers, the fourth Earl, was paying the penalty for murdering a steward who had charge of his family estates. But lesser people went to their deaths for the relatively minor crimes of picking the pockets of passers by, snatching purses or purloining a horse or a sheep.

High or lowly, they all made the three-mile journey from Newgate prison, which existed near the Old Bailey from the time of King John until 1902, to the gallows known as the Tyburn Tree near Marble Arch.

What a nightmare that journey must have been for them. All along the route, crowds fought and jostled to catch a glimpse of the condemned person in an open cart. Men, with too much drink inside them, lurched and staggered and passed beer to the prisoners. Old women, carrying clinking bottles in a basket, sold gin to the revellers who either ended up senseless in a doorway or, mad with drink, beat each other with sticks.

Nearer to Tyburn, the crowds were thicker and more boisterous. Apprentices and workmen playing truant swelled the throng that swarmed about the gallows. It was a holiday for them and for the people sitting in the specially erected stands, and for the wealthier patrons of the macabre who had paid dearly for choice seats at the windows and balconies of the surrounding houses.

All eyes were focused on the gallows. At first, from 1571 to 1759, this was a permanent structure of wood. Afterwards, until 1783 when hangings were transferred to New-gate, a movable gallows was used.

Lord Ferrers, it is said, had the honour of being hanged with a silken rope. For lesser mortals, the rope was made of a more common and coarser material. It was tied by the hangman. The earliest one known was named Derrick in James I's time. His successor was Gregory Brandon, the father of Richard Brandon who executed Charles I.

A hangman had to be tough and strong. If the crowd's sympathies were with the condemned man, they would sometimes try to rescue him from the gallows. This nearly happened in the case of Captain Kidd, a famous adventurer, who was found guilty of murder and piracy.

At the first attempt to hang him on 23rd May, 1701, the rope broke. Kidd, in a gold-brocaded gown, and helplessly drunk, staggered away from the gallows towards the crowd

Seeing the occupant of the coach waving and smiling at them, the watching crowd cheered. It was not every day that they saw a peer of the realm going to his execution.

who could have saved him. But he was too riotously intoxicated to co-operate with them. He was grabbed by the hangman and dragged back to the gallows, where he met his fate.

Sometimes, the victims would turn on the executioner. Two robbers, who had behaved in a tough way at their trial and sworn at the judge, set upon the executioner and knocked him out. They then called to the crowd to give them some wine, which some laughing spectators were happy to do. The men then drank the health of the Old Pretender, the Jacobite prince who had tried to claim the throne of Britain. When the executioner recovered consciousness, they were duly hanged.

However, some of the people who were sent to Tyburn would have been better served had the mob been sufficiently stirred up to save them. On some days at the beginning of the 19th century, batches of men, women and children numbering twenty or thirty were hanged for misdeeds which would have merited a fine, probation or a very short prison sentence today.

One of the victims in 1777 was a girl of 19 with a small baby. When her husband had been seized by a press gang and forced to become a sailor, this girl was left with no money at all. In desperation, she stole some cloth from a shop to make clothes for her baby. She was caught and ended her life at Tyburn.

Afterwards, her body was probably claimed by a "resurrection woman". This would have been one of a number of women who never missed an execution. They dressed in mourning and pretended to be a close relative of a victim. Their object was to obtain bodies for sale to laboratories, where students could use them for practising dissection.

Such grisly scenes were practically weekly occurrences during Tyburn's last hundred years until 1783, when the gallows was transferred to Newgate. Executions there remained public until they were put behind closed doors during Queen Victoria's reign.

The gallows at Tyburn was sold to a carpenter, who made it into stands for beer barrels for the cellars of a public house called the "Carpenter's Arms" in Adam Street.

And there, in time, it perished together with its infamous history.

For the condemned men on their way to the gallows, it must have been a nightmare journey, as the crowd fought to get a glimpse of them. The executioner was sometimes attacked by his victims but it made no difference—they usually met their fate in the end.

The second great FIRE of LONDON

Terror rained from the skies in the Second World War when London suffered a succession of bombing raids designed to bring the capital to its knees. But London survived, thanks to the courage of its inhabitants, the efficiency of the defence services and the bravery of the fire fighters.

Adolph Hitler, dictator of Germany during World War II, ranted at the officers of his High Command, ''Burn London!'' And with ruthless efficiency, the Nazis began to put his orders into operation.

Not since the Great Fire of 1666 had London been turned into such a burning conflagration as it was during the early years of the Second World War.

German bombers swept over the capital in waves night after night, setting acres of buildings ablaze. Warehouses, offices, homes, factories and ships in the docks succumbed to the fire-raising incendiary bombs that rained from the skies.

Hitler's intention was to bring Britain's capital to its knees to prepare the way for an invasion on 20th September, 1940. He very nearly succeeded, for plans were in existence for the evacuation of London. Had this gigantic operation been carried out, it would have been a shattering blow to the morale of the populace and to Britain's allies, and might even have lost the war.

However, London survived its sequence of

Scenes of devastation like this followed German air attacks upon London in the Second World War. The culprit, in this case, was a flying bomb.

raids and Hitler, instead of invading Britain, concentrated his forces on the Eastern Front where Russia was about to prove a formidable opponent to him.

London's survival was due to the courage of its inhabitants, the efficiency of all the defence organisations which protected it, and the bravery of the fire service.

The task of organising the capital's fire fighting forces was largely in the hands of Commander Sir Aylmer Firebrace, first as London's Regional Fire Officer and later as Britain's Chief of Fire Staff.

Before the war, London had 67 fire brigades. Commander Firebrace's job when he became Regional Fire Officer in 1939, was to weld these together into a unified force.

Large numbers of additional men and women were recruited into what became known as the Auxiliary Fire Service, to ensure that the force would be large enough to cope with the attacks which seemed inevitable.

The ammunition they were to use was water. And Commander Firebrace set about ensuring that plenty of this would be available. Underground mains, fed by diesel pumps from the Grand Union Canal, with hydrants at crucial points, were run under the city's streets.

Plans were also made to pump water from the Thames, ponds in the parks and swimming pools. Huge water tanks were built throughout the capital, and extra paddling pools for children were made in the parks so that water could be pumped from these. Swimming pools, too, were added to the list of places from where water could be obtained.

In a disused dry dock, an impregnable underground control room was constructed. From here, London's fire defences were to be controlled.

War was declared on 3rd September, 1939. For a long time, there were no attacks from the enemy. People objected to the expenditure of public money on the recruitment of extra firemen, who were kicking their heels in their stations or taking part in exercises which, to the spectators, seemed fruitless. Citizens complained about the emergency water tanks as being unsightly.

They were soon to change their opinions. In the autumn of 1940, London felt the full force of Hitler's fury. Between 7th September and 2nd November, London was bombed for 57 consecutive nights by forces of between 50 and 300 German bombers. And for the rest of that November there was an attack on all but three nights.

Some of the bombs they dropped were high explosives, but the vast majority were incendiaries which burst into flame as they hit the ground.

On each of these nights, London's skies turned red with the reflected glare of the fires that raged throughout the capital. Night after night, fire appliances sped through the rubble-strewn streets, finding their way by the light of the blazing buildings.

One of the main targets was the Surrey Commercial Docks. Here, ships blazed in the water, warehouses became acres of flame and the roads were bright with molten tar which flowed into bomb craters which they transformed into lakes of flames.

Faced with such an inferno, the fire service mustered all its resources. One fire officer sent an urgent message to his headquarters, "Send all the pumps you've got. The whole world's on fire."

As fast as one fire was controlled, another sprang to life. Stacks of timber, drenched with water from the firemen's hoses, burst into flames again when the water jets were directed on to a fresh outbreak. At one time, there were 42 huge fires raging in the docks, fought by 450 pumps!

When daylight returned after this particular raid, the firemen saw before them a smoking wilderness. What had been the Surrey Commercial Docks had become a ravaged desert of gutted warehouses and burning, blasted or sinking ships.

Certainly, the firemen and women deserved

Fires raged around St. Paul's Cathedral during the days of concentrated air raids, and the cathedral itself was damaged by fire which gutted the chapter house and by another bomb which pierced the dome and exploded inside the cathedral.

People salvage their furniture and other belongings from their wrecked homes after an air raid.

Among the important buildings to be hit by bombs was Buckingham Palace, which King George VI and Queen Elizabeth are examining here.

Rescue workers carry air raid victims away from the rubble of their demolished homes.

The fire fighters of Britain will never be forgotten as long as people have memories and appreciate that their courage has given us a heritage of peace which must always be preserved.

the 645 decorations for gallantry they received. Commander Firebrace described their plight in his book, "Fire Service Memories".

"When the whistle of a bomb was heard, most people in the streets could take cover," he wrote, "even if it were only to lie in the gutter or flatten themselves against a wall. Not so the fireman on an escape or one holding a branch on a roof, or the one at the head of a turntable ladder; he must just wait, sweating for what might be coming to him."

His fate could be to be blown through the air by an exploding bomb, killed, seriously injured or buried beneath the rubble of a collapsed building. Seven hundred fire fighters (including twenty women) were killed while trying to save London from destruction by fire. Seven thousand were seriously wounded.

London's last serious raid was on the night of 10th/11th May, 1941, when 300 planes dropped bombs which started 2,154 fires that damaged many important building, including the House of Commons. But the fire fighters got them under control with their customary skill and bravery.

The experience of London taught Britain a lesson which led to the birth of the National Fire Service in May, 1941 and brought Britain's one thousand fire authorities (town councils or county councils) into one vast body. It meant that the greatest number of fire fighters and their appliances could be concentrated upon the fiercest outbreaks of fire, wherever they occurred.

It was this vast force which fought the major enemy on the home front—fire! When peace returned, the force was disbanded, and the task of fire fighting was handed back to the local authorities. But while it existed, it was a formidable body of defenders whom, in the words of Winston Churchill written in 1945 when he was Prime Minister "must never be forgotten".

The fire fighters of Britain never will be forgotten as long as people have memories and appreciate that the sacrifices they made to save lives and property have given us a heritage of peace which must always be preserved.

Rubble litters a London street after a succession of air raids had rained terror on to the city.

Whether you use two fingers or all eight of them, a typewriter can speed up your writing tremendously

QWERTY. Is it a word? Is it a secret code? Is it someone's name, or something in a foreign language? If you were a typist, you would know that it is the first six letters on the top row of a typewriter keyboard.

"Why," you may ask, "are they in such a peculiar order? Why not arrange them alphabetically?" For the answer we have to go back to 1874 when E. Remington & Son produced the first practical typewriter.

Christopher Latham Sholes and his colleagues who invented the machine found in the initial stages that, even at comparatively slow speeds, the type bars clashed together. To overcome this they rearranged the keyboard so that the letters that occurred most frequently in the English language were positioned as far apart as possible. The resultant arrangement was

Christopher Latham Sholes who invented the first Remington typewriter which was sold in 1874. His machine is shown at the top of the page. On the right is the Imperial Model 'A' typewriter of 1908.

After Henry Mills' invention in 1714, nearly 160 years were to pass by before any significant advance was made.

substantially the same as that in use today.

The earliest record of a typewriter goes back to 1714 when Queen Anne awarded a patent to Henry Mills, an English engineer, for "an artificial machine or method for the impressing or transcribing of letters singly or progressively one after another, as in writing, whereby all writings whatsoever may be engrossed in paper or parchment so that the said machine or method may be of great use in settlements and publik records, the impressions being deeper and more lasting than any other writing, and not to be erased or counterfeited without manifest discovery".

But nothing else is known about Mr. Mills or his invention. There is no record of this machine having been made and no drawings or description of it.

Between 1714 and 1829 there were many other attempts to produce writing machines but none achieved more than a passing recognition. In 1829 William Austin Burt of Detroit invented the first machine to be registered with the American Patent Office—'The Typographer'. But it did not last for long. In 1836 there was a fire in the Patent Office that destroyed the only model.

Ideas for typewriters tumbled

An early 'portable' model, the Imperial Model 'D' of 1919.

from the fertile minds of many inventors in the following years, but it was not until 1873 that the forerunner of the modern machine made its debut. Sholes, a printer from Milwaukee, with Carlos Glidden and Samuel Soule, had some years previously worked on the development of a machine that would print consecutive page numbers in books. "Why stick to numbers?" asked Glidden. "Why don't we print letters of the alphabet?" And so they set to work to produce such a machine.

The three men approached

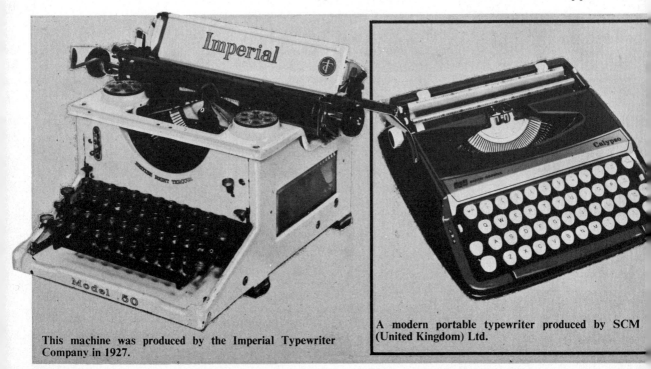

This machine was produced by the Imperial Typewriter Company in 1927.

A modern portable typewriter produced by SCM (United Kingdom) Ltd.

Just over one hundred years ago, in December 1872, Thomas A. Edison patented an electric typewriter but it was not until the late 1920s that an electrically powered machine became a practical proposition. Electric machines produce a more even impression than their manual counterparts thus ensuring a neater appearance to the typed page. They also cause less operator fatigue, and it has been calculated that an electric typewriter is at least 20% more efficient than a manual machine.

Some modern typewriters are worked by means of punched paper or magnetic tape which stores information in coded form. When the tape is fed into the machine the information is typed out at up to 180 words a minute.

The next development in typewriters could possibly be a voice-operated machine. All that will be required is for the writer to dictate into the machine and it will produce neatly typed work with no spelling mistakes and no alterations. A development that is a far cry from the day that Christopher Sholes, talking of his invention, shook his head and said, "You know that my apprehension is, that the thing may take for a while, and for a while there may be an active demand for them, but that like any other novelty, it will have its brief day and be thrown aside."

Remingtons, famous as gunsmiths and sewing machine manufacturers, with a view to producing the machine on a commercial scale. Twelve months later the 'Sholes and Glidden' was on the market.

The machine was made in the sewing machine section of the Remington works and this influenced its design. It was mounted on a base similar to that used for sewing machines of the period, and decorated with painted flowers, a common embellishment of sewing machines of that time. The carriage return was operated by a foot-treadle. Even the advertising brought in the sewing machine. The typewriter was described as a machine "the size of a sewing machine, and an ornament to an office, study or sitting room". It was predicted that the typewriter would become as "indispensable in families as the sewing machine".

Mark Twain, the popular author, was one of the first purchasers of the 'Sholes and Glidden'. It is claimed that he was the first author to use a typewriter and his book 'Life on the Mississippi' is believed to have been the first literary manuscript to be typed.

In a letter typed to his brother in 1875 he described the virtues of "this new fangled writing machine": "I believe it will print faster than I can write. One may lean back in his chair and work it. It piles an awful stack of words on one page. It don't muss things or scatter ink blots around. Of course it saves paper."

Later on Mark Twain found one disadvantage to owning a typewriter—the curiosity of his correspondents. He wrote to the Remington Company: "Please do not use my name in any way. Please do not even divulge the fact that I own a machine. I have entirely stopped using the typewriter, for the reason that I never could write a letter with it to anybody without receiving a request by return mail that I not only describe the machine but state what progress I had made in the use of it, etc., etc. I don't like to write letters, and so I don't want people to know that I own this curiosity breeding little joker."

Above: The IBM 'Electromatic', an early electric typewriter. At the foot of the page is a modern electric machine.

OUR WONDERFUL WORLD OF HISTORY QUIZ

How well can you remember the fascinating facts you have just learned in our History Section. Check your memory with the questions below.

1. Who found a way of preserving food in tins and is regarded as the father of the modern canning industry?

2. What did Heinrich Schliemann find in 1870?

3. Why were convicts taken to Tyburn?

4. Who was the Chief of Fire Staff in Britain in the Second World War?

5. Near which London church is there a plaque commemorating the first Punch and Judy show in England?

6. Where, apart from this page, can you see the letters QWERTY in that sequence?

7. Who was awarded a contract to carry mail across the United States in 1858?

8. What was the main business of Henry Wells and William Fargo?

9. Who discovered a way of preserving food in jars by heating it after the jar had been stoppered?

10. Dr. Alfred Taylor opened a can of meat at a lecture in London. How old was the can? What happened to the meat?

11. Who are the poets from whom we have learned about the wooden horse of Troy?

12. For what crime was Lord Ferrers hanged at Tyburn?

13. What did Hitler hope to do to Britain on 20th September, 1940?

14. What is the current name for the puppet, Pollicinella?

15. What did Christopher Latham Sholes invent in 1873?

16. In what country were travellers advised to carry a rifle, revolver and ammunition?

17. Who, besides the army and the navy, found canned food valuable in the early days?

18. How many cities were built, one upon the other, on the site of Troy?

19. What name was given to the women who claimed the bodies of the victims of the gallows at Tyburn?

20. In what year did Britain form the National Fire Service?

THE ANSWERS ARE AT THE BACK OF THE BOOK.

OUR WONDERFUL WORLD OF NATURE

WILD LIFE WONDERLANDS

In every part of the world, Nature, in all her forms, is being threatened by the activities of Man. As we continue to pollute the air, the soil, and the waters of the earth in our constant pursuit of technological progress, the natural habitats of animals and plants are rapidly disappearing. Where animals and plants once lived in the safety and freedom of wild, open countryside, giant factories and housing estates now stand, destroying the homes and food supplies of all kinds of creatures.

The only way to save the wild life of the world has been to set aside areas of land where animals and plants can live once again safe from the dangers of modern development and it was for this reason that National Parks, Nature Reserves and Sanctuaries were set up throughout the world.

But animals and plants are not the only ones to benefit from nature conservation. As more and more land is being developed to expand towns and cities, the areas of natural beauty become smaller and smaller. People now believe that there will soon be no wild life or wild country left in the world, except in National Parks and Reserves and these areas will soon be the only places where we can go to enjoy 'life in the country'. Since human beings seem to need to escape from the pressures of town life, these conservation areas will provide not only animals and plants with a chance of survival, but they will always help us to survive.

Today, every continent in the world has areas of land where people can enjoy watching wild life in natural surroundings. Let us take a look at some of these National Parks and Reserves.

JASPER NATIONAL PARK, ALBERTA, CANADA.

YELLOWSTONE PARK

The first national park to be founded was Yellowstone Park in the United States of America. This great wildlife area in the magnificent setting of the Rocky Mountains, covers 3,472 square miles and was set aside to preserve its beauty and animal life in 1872.

Among the many splendid sights in the park is the Grand Canyon, a huge gorge cut in brilliantly coloured rock by the Yellowstone River. Geysers and hot springs which occur all over the park, are other great attractions. One geyser, called Old Faithful, throws up its 140 ft high column of water every 65 minutes.

And amongst all this natural beauty in America's oldest and largest national park live the wild animals. Visitors can see black bear, mule deer, moose, bison, American elk, marmot, bighorn sheep and, occasionally, the grizzly bear. 200 species of birds are also protected in the area, and these include the bald eagle, and the rare trumpeter swan.

NAIROBI NATIONAL PARK

Almost 200,000 people visit this beautiful wildlife park in Kenya every year. The area covers 44 square miles and is divided into three separate zones. The western zone is thickly wooded, with groves of Kenya olives and flowering Cape chestnut; the central zone is a broad plain of grass and shrub, while the eastern zone contains many rivers and waterholes.

Across these zones roam lions, leopards, black rhinos, buffalo and zebra. Other wild creatures which inhabit the park include eland, gnu, Thomson's gazelle, Grant's gazelle, ostrich, marabou stork and crowned crane. There is even an animal orphanage for deserted and semi-tame animals.

KAFUE NATIONAL PARK

In the west-central part of Zambia lies Kafue National Park, a wildlife preserve which stretches for 8,650 square miles across a vast plateau which is larger than Wales.

The park is covered in lush, green vegetation, ranging from mixed forest, thicket, woodland and grass in the south, to broad, grassland and evergreen forest in the north.

A great number of fascinating animals inhabit the area. Buffalo, elephant and lion can be seen all over the park, and zebra, kudu, sable, crocodile and antelope are among the other animals which live there. The area is also rich in bird life, with openbills, cormorants, vultures, fish eagles and marabou stork.

HAWAII VOLCANOES NATIONAL PARK

This haven of wild life in Hawaii surrounds the active volcano systems of Mauna Loa and Kilauea. Mauna Loa is 13,680 feet high and pours forth hot lava every few years. On the slopes of the mountains hundreds of kinds of flowering plants and trees flourish in the Hawaiian climate. There are no large wild animals to be protected, but the park provides a sanctuary for feral pig, goat, mongoose, and native bats and rats.

One of the greatest attractions of the park is the population of fascinating birds. These include Japanese pheasant, California quail, nene goose, golden plover, pueo, chukar and Hawaiian hawk. The bird park contains 40 varieties of native trees and these include koa, ohia, soapberry, and kolea.

ENGLAND AND WALES

The national parks of England and Wales are much smaller than those in Africa and the U.S.A. As there are few wild animals in these countries, these parks serve mainly to preserve the beauty of the countryside for people to enjoy.

There are ten national parks in England and Wales: Peak District, Lake District, Snowdonia, Dartmoor, Pembrokeshire coast, North York Moors, Yorkshire Dales, Exmoor, Northumberland and Brecon Beacons.

THE LAKE DISTRICT

The mountainous parts of Lancashire, Westmorland and Cumberland make up the area called the Lake District. Between the mountains lie the valleys which contain the lakes. These include Windermere, Esthwaite Water, Coniston Water, Wastwater, Ennerdale Water, Derwentwater, Bassenthwaite, Thurlmere and the three linked together, Buttermere-Crummock Water-Loweswater.

The mountains, with trees and flowering plants on their lower slopes make it an area of scenic beauty.

SNOWDONIA

The mountainous area of Caernarvonshire in north Wales is called Snowdonia. It has more than 60 lakes, and many short, swift rivers which run from the mountains to the sea across the coastal plain.

Snowdonia National Park is an area of great beauty. Some of the rarest alpine flowers in Britain can be found in the Snowdon range and the area is a paradise for bird watchers. Ring ouzels, ravens, peregrines, buzzards and choughs are among the species of birds to be seen.

The area is also inhabited by pine martens and pole cats, and the rivers contain trout, otters and water voles.

Looking at LIZARDS

LIZARDS more closely resemble the prehistoric reptiles which once populated the world than do any of the snakes or alligators that we know today. Generally four-legged with scaly skins and long tails, they are found chiefly in the warmer parts of the world, although a few species survive in the north.

There are over 25,000 species of lizards in the world, and they have been grouped into about twenty families, half of which occur in the United States. At least 350 species have been found in North America.

A few species of lizard are snake-like in appearance, with long bodies and no traces of legs, but in other characteristics they resemble normal lizards and can be easily distinguished from snakes.

Most lizards have movable eyelids and some have an ear opening on the side of the head. Lizards also have the curious characteristic of being able to lose their tails easily and grow another one. When attacked by an enemy they simply leave their tails in the attacker's jaws and scuttle off. A new tail grows in about a month.

Most lizards lay eggs, but in a few cases, eggs develop inside the mother's body and the young are born alive.

All lizards can run extremely fast, the fastest having been known to reach 15 mph. Many of them can also swim, and a few can 'fly' from branch to branch with the help of outspread fans of skin.

A. DESERT CRESTED LIZARD

This handsome spotted creature lives in open desert, chiefly in burrows under sparse shrubs. It feeds on tender desert plants. It is reasonably large, being 12 to 15 inches long, and its tail is almost as long as its body.

B. LEOPARD LIZARD

Plump and spotted, the Leopard Lizard has a thin neck and narrow head. It prefers flat, sandy areas with some vegetation, feeding on insects and other lizards—often its own kind. The females lay two to four eggs which hatch in a month.

C. TURKISH GECKO

These geckos are most attractive. Their skin is usually covered by fine beaded scales and is almost transparent. They are easily recognisable by their large eyes, often with vertical pupils. Most of them have large, padded toes, and their tails break off easily. They are mainly nocturnal living around houses or in trees and feeding on small insects.

D. DESERT HORNED LIZARD

This odd and flattened creature is bizarre, with its various sized spines on its head. It is found in the western areas of America and Mexico, and also in Australia. At least eight species can be found in dry, sandy areas, where they lie on rocks or half buried in sand, flicking out their tongues to catch and eat passing insects such as ants.

E. FRINGED FOOT SAND LIZARD

This lizard's legs and fringed toes are long, and its tail is about body-length (six to eight inches), and often marked with black bars underneath.

F. GLASS SNAKE

Limbless and somewhat like a snake, the Glass snake's ear openings, eyelids and rows of belly scales proclaim it a true lizard. It is two to three feet long and its long tail breaks off more easily than most lizards, especially if roughly handled. The tail cannot rejoin, but a

new, shorter tail grows in its place.

G. ALLIGATOR LIZARD

Named for its shape and heavy scales, this is a slow, dull-coloured, solitary lizard with a banded or speckled back. It is fairly large, about ten inches, and some of the species lay eggs, while others give birth to young.

H. CLIMBING UTAS

These lizards prefer trees and rocks, where their dull colour gives them camouflage. Adults are small, five to six inches long, and males are a pale blue on the underside near the back legs.

I. COMMON WESTERN SKINK

Skinks are the widest range of lizard, but are poorly represented in the United States. Smallish, with a body of about five inches and a tail of about six inches, some have smooth, flat scales which give a glossy appearance. Most skinks are ground lizards and occasionally burrow with their short legs.

J. GILA MONSTER

This is a poisonous lizard. But the poison, from modified salivary glands in the lower jaw, is not injected and does not always enter a wound when the lizard bites. Two feet long, slow and clumsy, the Gila Monster can, however, twist its head, bite swiftly and hang on with its legs strongly. It lives in North America under rocks and burrows by day, feeding on eggs, mice and other lizards.

MIGHTY HUNTERS

As much at home in the water as any fish, the otter searches in rivers and streams for its prey.

WALKING along a river bank at night in late spring you may hear a shrill whistling and a lot of splashing.

These are sure signs that you are near an otter's holt or burrow and that the dog otter is busily catching fish while mother otter is teaching her young to swim.

Although otters are among the most expert of swimming animals, they do not swim naturally, but have to learn. In fact baby otters are frightened of water and their mother has to persuade them to go in.

One way she does this is to make a slide down the mud of the river bank. She then glides down this herself. The baby otters slide down after her and discover that the water is not so dangerous after all.

Once otters have learned to swim they are thoroughly at home in the water. Their short, powerful legs with the large webbed feet enable them to swim at a tremendous speed either on the surface or under the water.

They usually swim with their bodies just under the water and their noses above the surface. When they spot a fish they immediately dive after it. At the same time they close their ears to prevent water from entering.

An otter is able to hold its breath for quite a long time, so that it can swim under water for several minutes. Its body never gets wet or cold, for it has two coats: an outer waterproof one, and an inner one of thick, woolly fur.

Otters hunt eels, salmon, trout and pike. They vary this diet with an occasional swimming duck, which they catch by diving under the bird and pulling it down by its legs.

The otter belongs to a group of aquatic animals called *mustelidae*, and it is a close relative of the stoat and ferret.

The feeding habits of the Mustelids vary according to their environment and their habits. Some of them are fond of water and may catch a great many fish, others seldom see any large volumes of water and spend most of their life deep in the forest hunting rodents, such as mice. One thing that is quite clear in their feeding habits is that they are almost exclusively carniverous, and that they are all great hunters.

As far as is known, Mustelids are taught hunting at a very early age by their parents, this being an important part of their natural method of survival. The weasels, ferrets, badgers, etc., must also learn to defend themselves. None of the family is very large, the largest being the wolverines of North America, Canada and Northern Europe.

It is not unknown for members of the Mustelid family to become serious pests to farmers and live-stock breeders. Pine martens are known throughout Europe as killers of rabbits, hares, pheasants and partridges.

Otters will hunt in even the best kept rivers, and range the newly stocked water for young trout, having no regard for the Water Bailiff, who has spent a great deal of time and money raising the young fish for sporting purposes. It is not surprising therefore, that the hunters have become the hunted. Even dogs have been bred especially to hunt certain species and although only a limited amount of this type of hunting is carried on these days, nevertheless the breeds of dog are still in existence and Otterhounds and Dachshunds (Badger hounds), are both very popular breeds.

The Common Otter (*Lutra lutra*) is often referred to as the Old World Otter and is known throughout Europe, North Africa and Northern India. It grows to about 30 inches long, and its tail grows to about half this length, although the record length for the Common Otter is more than $5\frac{1}{2}$ feet. This specimen weighed more than 35 lbs., but generally they weigh about 20 lbs. Naturally enough, the otter's diet consists mainly of fish, but they are especially fond of eels. Otters are also known to hunt crayfish and water birds.

The Sea Otter, native to the Pacific coast of North America, lives on shellfish which it collects in its mouth from the seabed.

It has the remarkable trick of bringing up a flat stone, too, in its front paw. It then turns on its back to float, places the stone on its chest, removes the shellfish from its mouth with its paws and smashes them against the stone.

The cats came out to greet the cat's meat man at the same time every week.

NATURE'S ALARM CLOCKS

by DR. MAURICE BURTON

At the corner of a street in London a cat's meat man used to park his van at midday every Tuesday. He would throw scraps of meat to the cats assembled there. And every week, at a few minutes before twelve o'clock the cats would foregather there from the houses around, as if they knew what day it was and what time. This is only one example of the many things animals do that made people ask whether animals have a time sense.

People who keep a dog are struck by the regular way their pet keeps to a routine. One dog always went to the station to meet his master coming home by train. A few minutes before the train was due to arrive the dog would go to the gate and trot to the station, as if somebody had looked at the clock and told him it was time to go.

Farm animals know when it is feeding time, but this could be because all the sights and sounds around them act as guides. This might also be true of our dog. But it should be noted that this particular dog would not go to the station on Saturdays and Sundays, even if his master was away from home then.

At first there was no real answer to the question about a time sense. Then scientists began to talk about a biological clock. First one, then another, found that animals do certain things with the regularity of a clock. Some of these are done every twenty-four hours, others at weekly, monthly or yearly intervals.

On a sandy beach, at low tide, we see small piles of worm-castings made by a lugworm buried in the sand. The worm lives in a U-shaped burrow in the sand, swallowing sand and digesting any particles of dead matter in it. It must pass the sand out of its body and to the surface. Every 40 minutes, with great regularity the lugworm moves backwards up the burrow to add to the castings at the surface, then moves down again to continue forwards up the other arm of the U to take in more sand for feeding.

The lugworm makes these movements at 40-minute intervals no matter what is going on around it. Something inside itself tells it when it is time to make the movement —an internal 'clock'.

Other animals living on the shore have a rhythm of about 12 hours, corresponding to the rise and fall of the tide. Such animals are active when the tide is in and rest when the tide is out. When they are taken and put in an aquarium in which the level of the water remains the same all the time they still behave as if the tide were coming in and going out.

The internal alarm clock for them is a little more complicated because the times of high and low tide are slightly different each day, and the animal must adjust its movements accordingly.

There are certain fiddler crabs of the tropical beaches that go dark when the tide is out and become lighter in colour when covered with water. The change in colour is

114

Farm animals know when it is feeding time.

due to the contraction and expansion of cells in the crab's skin. When a fiddler crab is kept in an aquarium it changes colour in time with the rise and fall of the tide. More remarkable, if a piece of the crab's skin is removed and placed in a jar of sea-water it will still change colour in time with the tides!

At the other end of the animal scale there are the bats. They sleep by day hidden from the light and yet come out regularly each day at the right time for their evening's hunting.

The story is, however, the same for all animals, and to a large extent for plants as well. So we find that breeding seasons, whether these are in spring, summer or autumn, take place at regular times, so do migrations, the start of hibernation and the other processes of living. There can be slight differences in some of the dates, especially those where temperature is involved. But by and large there is for every living thing a regular time-table, and this is controlled in the first place by internal rhythms, although to some extent, external conditions take a hand.

We plant daffodil bulbs in autumn and they start then to throw out their roots. Later, the green shoot begins to grow and continues slowly to do so until the spring when it breaks through the surface of the soil. The actual day when this happens will depend on the temperature. A late winter will delay it, an early spring will bring it forward, but usually the difference in the end is only a matter of days.

On the whole it is the cycle of night and day that keeps the hands of the biological clock set correctly for the time of the year. Because this daily cycle is so important its rhythm is called the circadian rhythm, from the Latin words *circa*, meaning 'about', and *dies*, a day. Circadian then means about a day or roughly 24 hours.

Much has been learned about the biological clock and the circadian rhythm in the last quarter of a century, although a great deal more has yet to be found out. Through it we can understand many commonplace events that used to be puzzling.

Thus, birds start singing again in spring after having been silent during the winter. They also start courting. Then, curiously, after having been silent during July and August, following the moult, they begin to sing again in September, but not as strongly as in spring. They may even indulge in mild courtship in autumn, without actually mating. They do these things when the day-length, the number of hours of daylight, is roughly the same as when their singing and courtship begin in spring.

Light is, in fact, more important than anything else in setting the internal clock, as shown by experiments on cockroaches. These unwelcome insects come out in the evening searching for crumbs of food. Their activity reaches a peak about two o'clock in the morning, then wanes and about dawn the cockroaches retire to rest. This is quite regular.

When cockroaches are kept in total darkness for several days and nights their internal clock gets upset. They feed at all times of the day and night. They do the same amount of resting and searching for food, but it is scattered over the 24 hours.

If, now, they are exposed to a brief flash of light their habits go back to normal. They once again start to feed in the evening, reach a peak at 2 a.m. and cease to feed at dawn. What is more, they continue these regular habits even if once more kept in total darkness. The internal clock went wrong and it needed only a quick flash of light to put it right again. Moreover, it is not so much the flash of light as the sudden change from light to darkness that is needed.

This is very odd, but is only one among many odd features of the biological clock. One would have expected that once the cockroaches were back in the darkness the clock would go wrong again!

The fiddler crab goes lighter when covered in water.

EBENEZER

All day the big steam engine throbbed, driving the threshing machine which stood beside the wheat stack under the Dutch barn. One by one the sheaves of grain flipped onto the superstructure, and old Jenkins, with automatic skill, slashed the twine with his knife and fed the sheaves to the winnowing fan beneath him.

The whining note of the machine dropped and then lifted again each time it was fed. On the stack, above the machine young Jenkins flicked the sheaves accurately to his father, his pitchfork moving in perfect rhythm. Hour after hour went by, and inexorably the stack decreased, the pile of winnowed chaff grew, and the sacks of wheat went up the conveyor belt into the granary. It was a peaceful scene, common all over the countryside before the advent of the combine harvester.

A peaceful scene—but inside the diminishing stack there was fear and turmoil. In the foetid, airless runways the rats were stirring. They packed the tunnels as they scurried through them to avoid the men who were systematically destroying their fortress.

Ebenezer was the biggest rat in the whole colony. He was old and scarred, so old that his lower incisor teeth were curved backwards like miniature scimitars. He was a huge obese old gentleman with no manners. From the tip of his blunt muzzle to the end of his scaly tail, he measured twenty inches. Like all his kind he ate anything and everything that was edible, baby birds in their nests, meat and vegetables and corn. Horror of horrors, when driven by hunger, he was not averse to cannibalism.

As the wheat stack grew smaller, the swarming rats were in a frenzy of fear, and Ebenezer bit and tore at any of his companions who obstructed his progress.

The rats slithered hither and thither through the warm dark runways, squeaking and chattering. Some looked out into the stackyard and then retreated from the noise of men and machinery, and from the glare of the setting sun. The threshing machine hummed on, its noise rising and falling in the cool evening air.

Now the wheat stack was only two feet high. Suddenly it erupted. In ones and twos and then in a tumbling dark brown mass the rats fled. Men and boys stopped work, and with sticks, they laid about them. Dogs snapped and threw, and the dead rats twirled in the air. For every rat which lost its life, three escaped in the confused excitement. Some rushed straight into the pond, and swam to the safety of the boggy land beyond. They ran into drains and ditches, and went humpity hump across the darkening fields. They ran through gateways and over the low stone walls.

"Never seen the like of it," said old Jenkins. "Never in all my seventy years."

He stood on the threshing machine yelling like a banshee. He was in grave danger of falling into the idling winnowing fan beneath him. The opposite side of the stack was left unguarded, for the rats had followed one another in their headlong flight and the men, boys and dogs had gone to where the excitement was greatest.

Old Ebenezer, his long tail trailing, slipped from the side of the stack, and with his bloated stomach slithering across the ground he jumped into a deep stone drain, which led from the cowshed. He swam through the scum until he gained the main channel which led upwards to the farm buildings. Covered in black, clinging slime he crawled behind the oak panelling of the cow mangers.

Ebenezer, the old, the terrible, had escaped again. All his life he had been escaping death, death from weasels, stoats, men, ferrets, poison, traps, dogs, cats, hawks and owls and foxes. He had escaped from fire and flood.

There was the time when a lithe weasel had pinned him behind one ear. Usually that would be the end of any rat, but

An army of rats was on the move across the dark countryside, but no one knew why ... except, perhaps, old Ebenezer.

benezer, with his great strength nd weight, squealing with nortal fear, had rolled down the ank of a stream. He went deep wimming for his life, and the veasel was forced to release im.

By the same stream, a prowling tter had sprung from the rushes, nissing Ebenezer by a fraction of n inch as he dived into the bolt ole of a water rat.

Ebenezer had been caught in he teeth of a trap, and had scaped by gnawing off three es. It would seem that fat ncient Ebenezer was indestruct-le.

That night old Jenkins was eturning late to his cottage. He ad been to a whist drive in the illage Hall. The moonlit country-ide shone white with frost. awny owls were calling, and omewhere in the woods a fox ipped sharply. Old Jenkins aused to light his pipe, and en he stood like a statue, stening. From behind him came soft, sibilant, rustling sound. ld Jenkins turned to look back long the pale moon-washed ne between its dark hedgerows.

"Cor!", breathed the old man, nd hurried towards the lights of his cottage. He shut the door behind him carefully, and then ran upstairs to look through the bedroom window.

Like a brown unhurried flood which covered the lane from hedgerow to hedgerow, an army of rats was passing, jostling each other, furry bodies against furry bodies. Thousands of rats were on the move. Whither were they going? Why were they going?

No one will ever know. What had called them together? At the most there had only been two hundred rats in the wheat stack, and here were thousands. The massed army was safe, for no man, no predatory animal or bird would attack it. Thousands of bright eyes reflected the moon-light, moving like green jewels through the frosty night.

Ebenezer, long tail trailing, kept to the centre of the horde. It was safer there. Old Jenkins shivered.

"Cor!", he said.

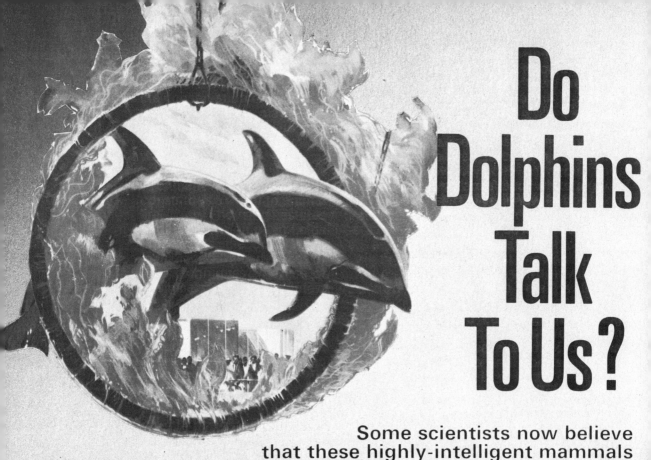

Do Dolphins Talk To Us?

Some scientists now believe that these highly-intelligent mammals do possess the power to communicate with human beings.

THERE is a story nearly two thousand years old about a boy who used to ride on a tame dolphin. The boy lived in the town of Hippo on the coast of Tunisia. He and his companions had a favourite game. They would let themselves be carried out to sea by the tide flowing out of a lagoon. One day the boy was carried away from the others, when suddenly a dolphin swam up to him. It swam around him and then dived under him, coming up again so that the boy was perched on its back.

The boy was frightened at first, but the dolphin carried him back to the beach. His story was soon passed around and on the next day a crowd gathered at the lagoon while the boys went swimming. Eventually the dolphin appeared and began playing around the swimmers. It allowed them to pat it, and the boy who had first met it found that he could climb on its back for rides.

The fame of the tame dolphin of Hippo spread far and wide and many people came to see it but the story had a sad ending. The people of Hippo were too poor to give hospitality to all the sightseers, so they killed the dolphin. We know this story because it was written down by the Roman historian Pliny. He thought that it was a true story, but for a long time people could not believe that a dolphin would make friends with a human in this way. Then, about 30 years ago, dolphins started to be kept in huge tanks of sea water called seaquaria or oceanaria.

Their keepers soon found that the dolphins were very tame and highly intelligent. They were easily taught tricks and people flocked to see performances by trained dolphins. At the same time scientists were using the captive animals to investigate their habits and their intelligence. Until dolphins were kept in seaquaria most of our knowledge about them was based on examining the bodies of dolphins which had been stranded on beaches. Now it became possible to study the live animals and to carry out experiments on them. The tame dolphins cooperated with the scientists and made their task much easier. Eventually, dolphins even gave birth in the seaquaria and the whole process of the birth and growing-up of baby dolphins could be watched through windows in the sides of the tanks.

The study of dead dolphins had revealed that they have large brains. This suggests that they must be intelligent. Some people even think that dolphins could be as intelligent as humans and that some day we may be able to talk with them. Other scientists do not believe that dolphins are that intelligent, but they are certainly more intelligent than dogs and probably as intelligent as chimpanzees.

Dolphins in the oceanaria are very quick at learning tricks. They will jump out of the water to ring a bell or take food from the trainer's hand, or will

jump through a paper covered hoop. Furthermore, a dolphin will strive to learn a trick. It will try again and again until it is satisfied with its own performance. Unfortunately for the trainer, when a trick is perfected, the dolphin is likely to get bored with repeating it. So the trainer has to make sure that there is a variety in the performance.

Apart from the pleasure of learning tricks from the trainer, dolphins will find their own games to play. One young dolphin teased a turtle that lived in the same tank by rolling it over like a hoop or tossing it out of the water with his snout. Another took pieces of food to the rock cranny where a grouper, a flesh-eating fish, lived. When the grouper came out to seize the food, the dolphin whisked it away. A group of dolphins in the Marineland oceanarium used to play tag. One would pick up a feather floating on the surface of the water, toss it in the air and catch it. Another would steal it and race off, chased by the others. Each would try to seize the feather and be chased in its turn.

The ease with which dolphins learn tricks has proved very useful when studying their senses. If, for instance, one wishes to find out how high-pitched a noise the human ear can detect, all one need do is to produce whistles of steadily higher and higher pitch with a special machine and ask volunteers at what point they can no longer hear them. To do the same with a dog, it is

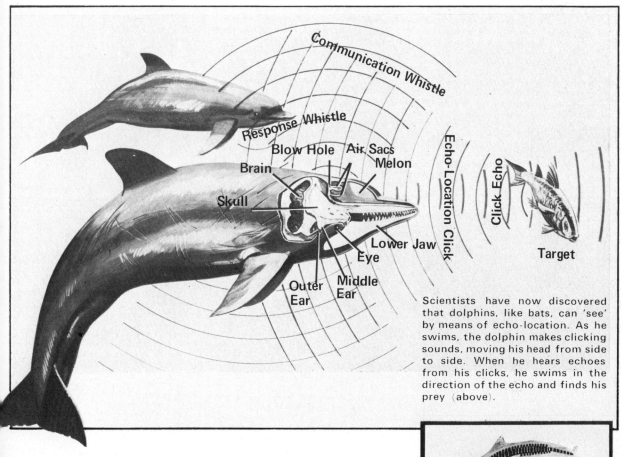

Communication Whistle

Response Whistle

Blow Hole   Air Sacs
             Melon

Brain

Skull

Echo-Location Click

Click Echo

Lower Jaw

Eye

Outer Ear   Middle Ear

Target

Scientists have now discovered that dolphins, like bats, can 'see' by means of echo-location. As he swims, the dolphin makes clicking sounds, moving his head from side to side. When he hears echoes from his clicks, he swims in the direction of the echo and finds his prey (above).

necessary to train the dog to respond when it hears a whistle. It can be trained to pull a lever, wag its tail or make some other signal. Then, the pitch of the whistle is raised and when the dog stops signalling, we know that the whistle has passed the highest pitch a dog can hear. Training a dog to respond when it hears the whistle may take some time but a dolphin learns quickly and appears to enjoy taking part in the tests.

The results of such experiments show that we can hear sounds of up to 20,000 cycles per second whereas dolphins can hear sounds with a pitch over six times as high, over 120,000 cycles per second. We are quite unable to hear these sounds and have to record them with special apparatus. The sounds are said to be ultrasonic, that is beyond the range of human hearing.

Exciting discoveries have come from the studies of the dolphins' power of hearing. It has been known for over 30 years that bats hunt insects at night by echo-location, or sonar. They emit ultrasonic squeaks and listen for the echoes that come bouncing back from nearby insects. Their powers of hearing are so good that they can follow an insect as it twists and turns in flight and they can detect and avoid wires almost as fine as a human hair that have been hung in their path. Now we know that dolphins, too, can hunt for fish in murky waters by mean of echo-location.

Right: A dolphin's spike-edged jaws can cut a fish in half with one bite. In the background are skeletons showing that the dolphin was once a land animal.
Below: A dolphin learns to imitate human sounds.

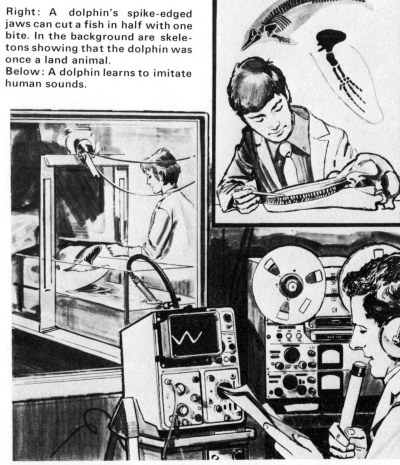

The first inkling that they had this extraordinary power came when it was found that dolphins were able to escape being caught in fishing nets even at night and in muddy water. The dolphins would charge at the net but, at the last second, would leap over it. They could not have seen it in the dark and, as it was already known that dolphins could hear ultrasonics, the scientists suspected that they might be using echo-location, like the bats.

The next step was to train a captive dolphin to come for fish in a tank of muddy water on a moonless night. The dolphin was called by slapping the water with a hand or by striking an iron pipe. It would come within 6 inches of the source of the noise from 20 yards away, which showed that its ordinary hearing was very good. But if there was no food it lost interest and swam away. When a fish was lowered into the water, the dolphin unhesitatingly picked it up. At the same time it was found that the dolphin was making noises like the creaking of a rusty hinge.

Each creak consisted of hundreds of tiny clicks. These were the sounds that it was sending out to detect food or obstacles, such as nets. The echoes coming back told the dolphin what was in the water in front of it.

Further experiments have shown just how good is the dolphin's power of echo-location. Dolphins have been trained to wear rubber cups over their eyes so that the experiments can be carried out during the day. Incredibly, it was found that one dolphin thus blindfolded was even able to distinguish between a lump of fish and a water-filled gelatine capsule of the same size by means of its echo-location.

Other experiments with tame dolphins have enabled scientists to study the way they swim and the way they can stay underwater for long periods. Sometimes the most interesting discoveries come by accident. At one oceanarium a dolphin was accidentally knocked unconscious. As dolphins are air-breathing mammals it could easily have drowned, but its two companions lifted it to the surface to breathe until it recovered.

Wild dolphins have also been seen rescuing an injured comrade. For thousands of years sailors have believed that dolphins will save men from drowning. We now know for certain that dolphins will rescue each other and, in 1943 an American woman was pushed back to the shore by a dolphin when she was drowning.

We have now come full circle. The Ancient Greeks knew that dolphins called to one another, that they would rescue injured comrades and occasionally, drowning men. They knew that dolphins were not fish, yet all these facts have been denied by later naturalists. Modern researches have shown that the Greeks were right. Even the story of the tame dolphin at Hippo has been shown to be more than a legend.

In 1955, a wild dolphin formed the habit of visiting the sea just off the town of Opononi in New Zealand. People soon found that it was very friendly and liked being scratched with an oar blade. Eventually the dolphin, nicknamed 'Opo', became so tame that she would come into the beach so that children could pat her and play with beach balls thrown to her. As at Hippo, centuries earlier, people flocked to see the tame dolphin. But at Opononi, the visitors were welcomed and the dolphin was protected. Unfortunately, there was another sad ending. A little more than a year after Opo had first appeared at Opononi, she was found lying dead. She had been trapped in a rock pool when the tide went out.

A trained dolphin swims to the rescue of a 'lost' diver, during an underwater experiment.

Watch-and save the birds

Observing birds and the way they behave can be one of the most interesting and rewarding of hobbies.

Everybody can enjoy the hobby of bird watching. It is not necessary to live in a vast area of open countryside surrounded by the beauties of nature to study these fascinating creatures of the animal world. There is a bird population just as varied and

Wren

Robin

Blackbird

Blue tit

Chaffinch

Song thrush

interesting in the heart of a bustling, overcrowded city, and wherever there are parks with trees you will find birds to watch.

If you have good eyesight, a keen sense of hearing, and a lively interest in everything which goes on about you, you are already off to a good start in your new hobby. And if you are an expert at hide-and-seek, so much the better, because your experience and skill at moving quietly and unseen will be invaluable when you are watching birds.

You can begin by trying to identify the birds which you see everyday; on your way to and from school, in the park, or in the garden. A well-illustrated book on British birds will be a great help, so a visit to your local library to borrow a colour picture book on birds is one of the first things you should do.

Every bird watcher needs a notebook in which to jot down notes and quick sketches of the birds seen. This is really the only way you can make an accurate identification of a bird at first. It is sometimes difficult to identify the most common birds when you begin. Many people, for example, mistake a starling for a blackbird.

At first, you will probably be able to observe and identify many birds with the naked eye, but if you become very interested in your new hobby, and intend to take it seriously, you may want to buy a pair of binoculars. But if you decide not to, or if you cannot afford a pair, so much the better. You will become a much more proficient ornithologist without them, for you will have to learn to recognise birds by the way they fly, and their shape and size from a distance.

It will also teach you to rely on the songs and calls of birds to make your identification. This is a very import-

Buzzard and young

A kingfis[h]

DATE: September 1973
TIME: 2.30 pm.
PLACE: Yorkshire Moors.
WEATHER: Dull, Slight Rain, Cold
HABITAT: Wild Moorland
DISTANCE: 20 Yards
NUMBER: Six
CALLS + Short Tweets—One long
SONGS: then short, staccato notes
ACTION: All flying gracefully,
darting and diving, flying
low over moorland
CONCLUSION: SWALLOW

Red   Blue   Forked Tail   White Under parts

ant means of identifying birds because sometimes you will not have the opportunity to see a bird, but only to hear it. The nightingale, for example, often lies hidden in a tangle of undergrowth and cannot be seen, but its song is unmistakable.

Should you decide to buy a pair of binoculars, great care must be taken in choosing a good pair. A brand new pair of poor quality binoculars are useless. It is better to buy a secondhand pair made by a reputable, well-known firm which will be the same price as the 'cheap' brand new pair.

Make sure that the binoculars you choose are focused by means of a central wheel, and can be adjusted by a slight movement of the fingertips—not one in which

both eye pieces have to be adjusted separately. The most suitable and most frequently used for bird watching are: 7 x 50 and 8 x 40.

Binoculars are classified by two numbers. The first is the number of times the picture is magnified, and the second number is the diameter of the object-lens in millimetres. You may want to achieve a very strong magnification—say 10 times—but this is not always wise because, although you will get a bigger picture of your subject from further away, the image will be fuzzy and will require much more focusing every time the bird moves.

On your first day as an amateur bird watcher, then, you will set out armed with your bird spotter's notebook and pencil, binoculars if you

Female mallard on a nest in an old tree stump

have them, and your eyes and ears as alert as those of a fox on the prowl.

As soon as you catch sight of a bird, you must start sketching a rough drawing of it in your notebook, and then enter some detailed notes: Take care to note the colour of the plumage on all parts of its body. Has it a black patch on its head? Pink underparts? Red legs? All these will help you to identify it accurately. As soon as you get home, you can then compare your notes with the descriptions of birds in your book.

It is a good idea to keep a special notebook at home in which you can copy and write up your quick notes. In this way you will have a permanent well-kept record of all the birds you have seen over a long period of time. A loose-leaf file to which pieces of paper can be added is ideal for this purpose.

When you are not actually 'out in the field' carrying out the practical side of your hobby, you can begin to read about the habits of birds you have seen, so that all the time you are developing a deeper knowledge of their behaviour. The day when you see a drake mallard lift one of its wings, preening itself in front of a duck, and realise that he is performing part of a highly ritualised courtship display will be the day on which you know you have become a real bird watcher.

By recognising habits like these, you have proved that you can not only identify different birds, but can also *interpret* their behaviour. It is at this stage that the study of birds becomes a study of a whole way of life. You can start a special project of your own. Observing the life cycle of one particular type of bird; noting all the changes in shape, size, colour and behaviour that take place as a bird grows up.

You may want to keep a visual as well as a written, record of this, so photography will come in here as well. Or perhaps it is the songs of different birds that really fascinate you. If this is the case, you can make a detailed, intensive study of the calls and songs of one species of bird, recording them on a portable tape recorder, and finding out how they differ according to the time of year and habitat.

Whatever specialised interests you have in birds, there are endless possibilities of studying them, and it is up to you to decide which particular aspect of bird life interests you most. One thing is for certain. If you get to the stage of taking a specialised interest in bird behaviour, you may be sure that your hobby of studying them will bring you constant enjoyment and amusement.

Once you have become a serious bird watcher you will probably become very interested in the problem of wild life conservation and threats to bird life. You may even feel moved to help in the saving of birds in a practical way.

Every change in his environment which Man makes constitutes a threat to animal life. New housing estates and buildings on open fields and heaths, the draining of marshlands; the advances of farm techniques; the use of chemicals; and the latest menace of waste oil from tankers, have all taken their toll on bird population.

Fortunately, much has been done in recent years to protect birds and to save their habitats. Organisations have been set up in order to set aside areas where birds can live safely. Today, there are reserves all over Britain which have been set up by the Nature Conservancy, national organisations, and local societies.

The County Naturalists' Trusts now cover every county in England and Wales. (In Scotland they are represented by a central Wild Life Fund.) The aim of these trusts is to conserve wild plants, animals, and their habitats. They organise nature trails, field museums, lectures, and exhibitions.

The Royal Society for the Protection of Birds own some of the most important nature reserves in Britain. It has an educational branch which arranges courses for adults and children in many parts of the country. It also runs its own club for young people—The Young Ornithologists' Club. If you would like to belong to this club, the address to write to for details of membership is:

Royal Society for the Protection of Birds,
The Lodge,
Sandy,
Bedfordshire.

A Peep Into a Pond.

One of the most interesting ways of observing nature at work is to visit a pond, for there you will find all kinds of strange and fascinating forms of life to study.

IF you have never been pond fishing and think that only a few frogs and newts live in them, you would be very surprised at what you could find. All ponds, whether they are large or small, are teeming with strange and fascinating forms of life for you to discover. This makes a study of a pond life one of the most interesting and rewarding of hobbies.

There are many plants and animals which flourish in, on, or around a pond. Willows, sallows, poplars and alders are all damp-loving trees and bushes which grow happily near the water's edge. Animals, like the water vole and water shrew thrive in ponds, and there are some very interesting birds that nest in trees and bushes nearby. Some, like the dabchick, raise their young on floating nests of dead plants on the surface of a pond.

But what about the plants and animals that live IN the pond? First of all, there are, of course, the amphibians such as frogs, toads and newts. If you visit a pond during springtime you will probably see frog spawn on the water surface, floating like big blobs of jelly.

The spawn of the toad is not always so noticeable because it is laid in strings round water weeds. You would have to look even more closely to find the spawn of newts because these are laid one by one, or in groups on water weeds.

All the eggs, though, hatch into tadpoles which live in the pond. Tadpoles breathe by means of gills at this stage. When they have turned into adults they breathe by sucking air into the mouth through two nostrils by lowering the throat. Then the nostrils are closed, and, by lifting the throat, air is pushed into the lungs. This is one of the most remarkable features of the frog and you can actually see this breathing process taking place by watching the frog's throat pumping up and down all the time.

It would be very difficult to find a frog in wintertime. At this time of the year it plunges into the mud at the bottom of the pond and stays there until spring comes, when it rises to the surface again to breed and lay eggs. This, by the way, is the best time to hear the famous croaking sound which frogs make.

Catching tadpoles to take home and study can be very interesting, but there are many more fascinating pond creatures which can be just as much fun to study. If you decide to build up a pond-life aquarium at home or a pond in your garden, an outing to a pond is essential. There, you will find the kind of

1. The hatching of a damsel fly from a nymph. 2. A newt and its spawn.
3. A pond skater. 4. A great water beetle. 5. A whirligig beetle.
6. A frog and its spawn.

conditions which your future pets live in, and if you are to make a success of your study you must always try to create a home for these creatures which is as near as possible like their natural environment.

Before you set off, take with you a large, strong pond net, some jam jars and a magnifying glass. With the net you can catch all kinds of pond creatures by simply sweeping the net through the water and then placing them in jam jars of pond water ready to take home.

Water insects are fascinating to watch because they can walk on the surface of the water without getting wet. This is because there is a very fine film on the surface which light insects can stand on. Good insects to catch include water measurers, water gnats and the delightfully-named pond skaters, who dart across the water with great agility.

Blue-black whirligig beetles are great fun to watch because they spin round and round at a very high speed. The water boatman deserves the title of pond swimming champion. This insect is an expert swimmer and diver. The larger water boatman, *Notonecta*, is boat-shaped and swims upside down and the smaller, flatter *Corixa* swims with its back uppermost. Both use their flattened, hairy legs as a pair of oars to propel their bodies along.

Another swimmer is the great water-beetle which swims with hind legs shaped like paddles. It is also a very strong flier, but beware of catching this insect. It is so dangerous to other forms of pond life that you must never place it in a tank or jar with other creatures.

Water spiders are delightful creatures. They live under the water and bring their air down with them. They make beautiful bell-shaped webs among the pond weeds and swim down from the surface with air bubbles entangled in the hair of their bodies. These underwater bells are the water spiders' homes where they eat, rest, and bring up their off-spring.

There are large amounts of the larva of insects living in ponds. Beetle larva and mosquito larva, live under the water and breathe the oxygen from aquatic plants. Tiny crustaceans can also be caught in ponds. They can be seen more clearly with a magnifying glass. One of these, *Daphnia*, jerks about the water like a little flea.

1. Floating duckweed. 2. Water snails. 3. Goldfish.
4. Anarcharis. 5. Vallisneria. 6. Sagittaria.

Perhaps the most interesting creatures to watch are the nymphs. These are the larvae of dragonflies, damsel-flies, and mayflies. They spend many months under the water, and when they are ready to shed their outer cases and emerge as adults, they climb up a support (perhaps a plant growing in the water), and then wait until the case begins to split. If you are lucky enough to catch a nymph you can watch this fascinating process yourself.

Finally, on your visit to the pond you may be lucky enough to see one of nature's most beautiful sights : a shimmering dragonfly hovering above the water, the rays of the sun lighting up its transparent, delicate wings.

How To Build A Pond

If you would like to build a pond in your garden, first ask your parents whether they will allow you to build one and also, whether they will be willing and able to help you.

Building a garden pond is not quite as difficult as many people believe. Gone are the days of hard, back-breaking work, mixing sand and cement to line the pond. Digging the hole, though, can be fairly tiring. It is always best to dig a shallow part at one end and to make the deep end about 18 inches deep.

Once the hole has been dug, the pool has to be lined. Plastic sheeting is most suitable because this will not be damaged by frost. You can obtain plastic sheeting from gardening shops or shops which specialise in water gardens.

The size of sheet you will need depends, of course, on the measurements of your pond. The LENGTH is the length of the longest side of the hole plus twice the maximum depth. The WIDTH is the width of the widest part of the pool plus twice the maximum depth. If, for example, the hole is 7 feet by 5 feet with a maximum depth of 18 inches, the size of the sheet you will need will be : 7 feet plus $1\frac{1}{2}$ feet plus $1\frac{1}{2}$ feet (10 feet long). 5 feet plus $1\frac{1}{2}$ feet plus $1\frac{1}{2}$ feet (8 feet wide).

The plastic sheet should be laid over the hole and weighted down with heavy stones around the edges. Then the pool must be filled slowly from a hose so that the plastic sinks to the bottom. After it is filled, the sheeting must be trimmed round the edges. Leave at least six inches all round so that the edges can be covered with stones to keep plastic in place.

You may, of course, prefer to buy one of the many ready-made ponds of moulded fibre glass, but these would be more expensive.

The pond should now be left for several weeks to allow it to 'settle down'. After a few weeks microscopic animals will float into the pond to aerate the water and later, provide food for the inhabitants of the pond. While you are waiting for the pond to be ready, you can start selecting the plants you would like in it.

There are three main kinds of water plants suitable for ponds : (1) Underwater pond weeds. These include starwort, curled pondweed, anarcharis, and water crowfoot, and they help to keep the water clean and aerated. (2) Surface plants : These include the beautiful water lily which provides shade. (3) Decorative plants : Forget-me-nots, marsh marigolds, arum lilies and reeds. These are all waterside plants which can decorate the borders of the pond.

After about three weeks you can then put in wate

snails, and many of the water insects which we have already mentioned in our look at pond life.

Once you have stocked your pond with these creatures you can then wait and see which animals come to visit your pond. Many of them may wish to make their home there and perhaps a good-natured frog will come along, bringing with him his wife, to start a family.

Whether you decide to build up a pond-life aquarium or a garden pond, it is always best to obtain a book about the subject where you will find advice on how to look after them all the year round.

A Pond-Life Aquarium

Now that you know what to look for at the pond, and what sort of conditions pond creatures live in, you may wish to build an aquarium for them at home. First, there are four very important rules for aquarium-keepers to observe:

1. The water in the tank must be kept fresh and clean. It must also be aerated (contain tiny bubbles of air).
2. Never overcrowd the inhabitants of the aquarium.
3. Never overfeed them.
4. Make sure that the creatures which you want to keep will live peacefully together. This means that you will have to know whether they are likely to fight or eat each other!

The choice of tank is very important. Goldfish bowls with their narrow necks are the WORST POSSIBLE type of home for your new pets. The tank should be made almost entirely of glass, rectangular in shape, and long and wide. A glass cover raised on bits of wood or cork at each corner will prevent dust falling into the water, and at the same time allow plenty of air to enter the tank.

Once the tank is bought, it should be washed thoroughly and the bottom lined with a layer of coarse sand, about 2 inches deep. Before you fill the tank itself, first fill a bucket with ordinary tap water and leave it outside in the open for a few days This will aerate the water and allow tiny animals which live in the air to float into the water. These are called infusoria and they, too, help to aerate the water.

Now you are ready to fill the tank. Place a saucer on the layer of sand and pour the prepared water gently on to it. This prevents the sandy bed from being disturbed.

Next, put in a variety of water plants. They can be bought in pet shops. Ask for Vallisneria, Sagittaria and Anarcharis and be sure to follow the planting instructions very carefully. You can also put some floating duckweed into the tank, and freshwater snails which help to keep the water clean.

You may decide that a few goldfish will be just the thing to complete the tank. Be very careful when moving a fish from one receptacle to another. You must make sure that the temperature is the same in both because fish are easily chilled. With a tiny net, lift out the fish and gently place it into the tank.

The aquarium we have described is suitable only for cold-blooded fish, not tropical fish. To give you a very rough idea of how much it will cost to set up a pond-life aquarium, an average-sized tank costs about £3·00. This, together with water plants, sand, goldfish and other creatures, will bring the total cost to approximately £4·00 to £5·00.

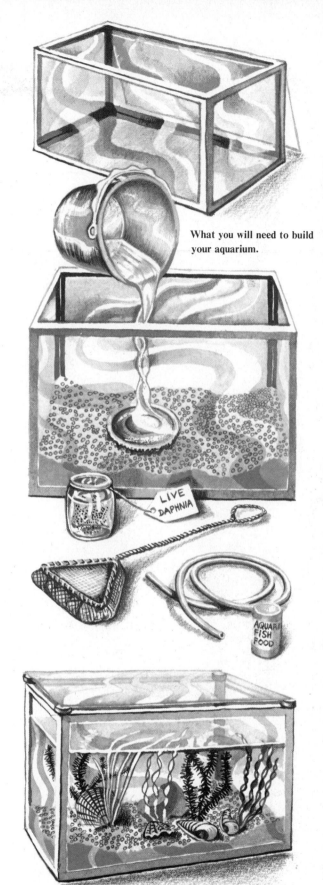

What you will need to build your aquarium.

A simple fish tank in your home can be an ideal way to study nature.

OUR WONDERFUL WORLD OF NATURE QUIZ

Now that you have read the articles in our Nature section, here are some questions for you to answer. You can find out how much you have learned by seeing how many questions you can answer correctly.

1. Name the first national park to be founded. When was it established?

2. Where, in Africa, is Nairobi National Park?

3. Kafue National Park lies in which African state?

4. How many national parks are there in England and Wales?

5. The mountainous parts of Lancashire, Cumberland and Westmorland make up an area of England. What is this area called?

6. Where is Snowdonia?

7. Why is the leopard lizard so called?

8. What is particularly unusual about the appearance of the Desert Horned Lizard?

9. What is unusual about the glass snake?

10. Is the Gila Monster a poisonous or non-poisonous lizard?

11. There are about 20 families of lizards in the world. Can you give an approximate number of species of lizards which are found in the world?

12. What do we call the method by which dolphins can 'see'?

13. The rhythm of the daily cycle in animal life is called the circadian rhythm. What does 'circadian' mean?

14. How do adult frogs breathe?

15. What are the eggs of frogs called?

16. Which season of the year is the best time to hear the famous croaking sound which frogs make?

17. What is remarkable about water insects?

18. What are the larvae of dragonflies, damselflies, and mayflies called?

19. Is a goldfish bowl with a narrow neck suitable as a home for pond creatures?

20. Floating duckweed and freshwater snails perform a very important function in aquariums. What do they do?

THE ANSWERS ARE AT THE BACK OF THE BOOK.

QUIZ ANSWERS

OUR WORLD QUIZ

1. The Severn bore. 2. France. 3. A bore on the River Amazon in Brazil. 4. Cambodia. Angkor Wat. 5. Driver ants. 6. In 1960. 7. In 1431 or 1432. They left no records apart from the temples. 8. In 1722. 9. Enormous, identical statues. 10. Rapu. 11. Colorado. 12. An international reply coupon. 13. Commander Holbrook. 14. Red Indians. 15. A boomerang. 16. The war boomerang and the return boomerang. 17. Plastic or steel. 18. "Pioneer". 19. More than a foot. 20. The twelfth century.

ARTS QUIZ

1. Augsburg, Germany. 2. The Doom Window. 3. Richard Wagner. 4. Senta and the Dutchman. 5. Frankenstein was the name of the scientist who is supposed to have created the monster. 6. Mary Wollstonecraft Shelley. She thought up the idea when making up ghost stories with her friends in Switzerland. 7. Boris Karloff. 8. 'The Addams Family' and 'The Munsters'. 9. Painting with water. 10. Paul Sandby. 11. London. His father was a barber. 12. Rain. 13. Two halves of a coconut shell knocked together (or plastic bowls). 14. Lord Byron. 15. King of Assyria. 16. Samuel Langhorne Clemens. 17. Hannibal. 18. The Mississippi. 19. To become a riverboat pilot on the Mississippi. 20. *Innocents Abroad.*

SCIENCE QUIZ

1. Sea shells. 2. Hollow cavities such as the middle ear and the lungs. 3. Nitrogen. 4. Liquid. 5. A sandwich of several layers of toughened glass. 6. Operates a boiler. 7. The Space Shuttle. 8. The Orbiter. 9. Coal and petroleum. 10. Measurements of heat. 11. Hydrogen and carbon. 12. Nuclear fuels. 13. Ergs. 14. Meteorites. 15. About 150. 16. Nickel-iron. 17. Microscopy. 18. A microscope. 19. The electron microscope. 20. Electrons. Sir J. J. Thomson.

HISTORY QUIZ

1. Bryan Donkin. 2. Troy. 3. To be hanged. 4. Commander Sir Aylmer Firebrace. 5. St. Paul's church. 6. On a typewriter. 7. John Butterfield. 8. Banking. 9. Nicholas Appert. 10. Twenty years. It was eaten. 11. Homer and Virgil. 12. For murdering a steward. 13. Invade it. 14. Punch. 15. The typewriter. 16. The United States in the 19th century. 17. Explorers. 18. Nine. 19. Resurrection women. 20. 1941.

NATURE QUIZ

1. Yellowstone Park. 1872. 2. Kenya. 3. Zambia. 4. Ten. 5. The Lake District. 6. In the mountainous part of Caernarvonshire in north Wales. 7. It is a spotted lizard. 8. It is a flat shape with various sized spines on its head. 9. It has no limbs. 10. The Gila monster is a poisonous lizard. 11. Over 25,000 species. 12. Echo-location. 13. About a day, or 24 hours. 14. By sucking air into the mouth through two nostrils by lowering the throat. The nostrils are then closed and, by lifting the throat, air is pushed into the lungs. 15. Spawn. 16. Spring. 17. They can walk on the surface of the water without getting wet. 18. Nymphs. 19. No, because the narrow neck does not allow enough air to enter the tank. 20. They keep the water clean.